"As credit default swaps become ever more important as a bank risk-management tool, so market participants will need to understand the credit market cash-synthetic basis. This is an excellent treatment of the subject that provides valuable detail for investors and traders alike."

  —MOHAMOUD BARRE DUALEH
  Abu Dhabi Commercial Bank

"Professor Choudhry turns the complexities of the credit market synthetic-cash basis from a probing delivery in the corridor of uncertainty into a juicy half volley. An excellent account and one sure to be of inestimable value to market practitioners."

  —MARK BURGESS
  Synthetic ABCP Operations, KBC Financial Products

THE

CREDIT DEFAULT SWAP

BASIS

Also by Moorad Choudhry

Fixed-Income Securities and Derivatives Handbook:
Analysis and Valuation

Also available
from Bloomberg Press

Inside the Yield Book:
The Classic That Created the Science of Bond Analysis
by Sidney Homer and Martin L. Leibowitz, PhD

The Securitization Markets Handbook:
Structures and Dynamics of Mortgage- and Asset-Backed
Securities
by Charles Austin Stone and Anne Zissu

PIPEs: A Guide to Private Investments in Public Equity
Revised and Updated Edition
edited by Steven Dresner with E. Kurt Kim

Hedge Fund of Funds Investing:
An Investor's Guide
by Joseph G. Nicholas

Market-Neutral Investing:
Long/Short Hedge Fund Strategies
by Joseph G. Nicholas

———————

A complete list of our titles is available at
www.bloomberg.com/books

THE

CREDIT DEFAULT SWAP

BASIS

Moorad Choudhry

BLOOMBERG PRESS

NEW YORK

BLOOMBERG, BLOOMBERG LEGAL, *BLOOMBERG MARKETS*, BLOOMBERG NEWS, BLOOMBERG PRESS, BLOOMBERG PROFESSIONAL, BLOOMBERG RADIO, BLOOMBERG TELEVISION, BLOOMBERG TERMINAL, and BLOOMBERG TRADEBOOK are trademarks and service marks of Bloomberg L.P. All rights reserved.

This publication contains the author's opinions and is designed to provide accurate and authoritative information. It is sold with the understanding that the author, publisher, and Bloomberg L.P. are not engaged in rendering legal, accounting, investment-planning, or other professional advice. The reader should seek the services of a qualified professional for such advice; the author, publisher, and Bloomberg L.P. cannot be held responsible for any loss incurred as a result of specific investments or planning decisions made by the reader.

The views, thoughts, and opinions expressed in this book are those of the author in his individual private capacity, and should not in any way be attributed to KBC Financial Products or KBC Bank N.V., or to Moorad Choudhry as a representative, officer, or employee of KBC Financial Products or KBC Bank N.V.

Certain material in this book has been published previously in the *Journal of Structured Finance* 11, no. 4 (Winter 2006); the *Journal of Derivatives Use, Trading and Regulation* 10, no. 1 (June 2004); *Structured Credit Products: Credit Derivatives and Synthetic Securitisation* (John Wiley & Sons Asia, 2004); *Professional Perspectives on Fixed Income Portfolio Management*, Volume 4, edited by Frank Fabozzi (John Wiley & Sons, 2003); and *Derivatives Week* (Euromoney Publications, December 2, 2001). Material reproduced with permission.

First edition published 2006
1   3   5   7   9   10   8   6   4   2

Library of Congress Cataloging-in-Publication Data

Choudhry, Moorad.
   The credit default swap basis / Moorad Choudhry.
       p. cm.
   Includes bibliographical references and index.
   ISBN-13: 978-1-57660-236-2 (alk. paper)
   ISBN-10: 1-57660-236-2 (alk. paper)
1. Credit derivatives. 2. Swaps (Finance) 3. Default (Finance) 4. Basis (Futures trading) I. Title.

   HG6024.A3C4922 2006
   332.63'2--dc22   2006048420

For one last time…
—Leeds Permanent Building Society, 1994

or

No thanks to anybody…
—Felt, *Gold Mine Trash* (Cherry Red Records, 1987)

CONTENTS

EXPANDED CONTENTS

FOREWORD

During the past few years, the credit derivatives market has grown significantly and is now an established derivative market. This market has given some investors a choice on how they should take exposure to the credit risk of a company—either via a credit derivative contract or by buying/selling the bonds of that company. The CDS contract (credit default swap contract) is the building block to many exotic credit derivative structured products and indexes. The CDS is a contract that is designed to pay out if there is a credit event affecting the reference credit.

The subject of examining the cash-CDS basis and answering questions such as why it exists, how to measure and monitor the basis, and how to react to changes in the measure and understand relative value are key questions for all credit investors.

Moorad Choudhry has written this timely, insightful, and accessible book about the cash-CDS basis that combines his in-depth academic knowledge with his own excellent skills as a market practitioner. It deserves a wide readership.

—RICHARD PEREIRA
Vice President, Structured Alternative Investments
J.P. Morgan Securities Ltd.

PREFACE

This is a book about the credit default swap basis. It is *not* a book about credit default swaps, much less a book about credit derivatives, a subject that is the focus of a great many books these days.[1] Of course it closely concerns credit default swaps—or rather, one particular aspect of their trading, analysis, and performance—and so readers should be familiar with the credit default swap (henceforth CDS) as a financial instrument. But it is not a book about the CDS *per se*. It is about an aspect of CDS behavior that is, whether appreciated by them or not, of importance to all users of CDS products. This is the *basis*, which can be loosely defined as the relationship between the cash and synthetic credit markets.

A basis exists in all markets where cash and derivative forms of the same asset trade side by side. For example, there is a crude oil basis, and a government bond futures basis. Put simply, the basis is the difference in price between the cash form of an asset and the price of that asset when represented by a derivative contract written on that asset. Depending on the type of asset

---

1. I particularly recommend *Credit Derivatives* (Mark Anson et al.); *The Handbook of Credit Derivatives* (Mark Francis et al.); *Credit Derivatives* (Geoff Chaplin); and *Credit Derivatives, CDOs and Structured Credit Products* (Satyajit Das). Readers will have to judge for themselves if *Structured Credit Products* (Moorad Choudhry) has the right to be in this esteemed company!

we are talking about, whether financial or physical, the basis will have a value that it *should* be. However, various factors combine to make the basis move away from its theoretical value, and it is this divergence that is of importance to market participants. Why is the credit default swap basis important? Because it is the measure by which investors—indeed, all market participants—can assess relative value in the credit markets, for both cash bonds and CDSs. The relationship and interplay between the two markets is captured in the basis. Thus, the basis becomes the key measure of relative value for credit-risky assets, as well as an indicator of mispricing of these assets, whether they are in cash or synthetic form.

The use of interest-rate derivatives increased liquidity in the world's financial markets. Such instruments made it easier for users and providers of capital to price and hedge cash market debt capital products. Interest-rate swaps are now a leading indicator in the financial markets and a tool by which cash market efficiency is maintained. We can observe a similar development occurring in credit markets. Credit derivatives were introduced around 1994, although a liquid market did not develop until a few years after that. They are now an important part of the global capital markets, and have contributed to increased liquidity in the cash credit market. They also enable market participants to price credit as an explicit asset class.

As the synthetic market in credit becomes a reliable indicator of the cash market in credit, mirroring the development in interest-rate markets a generation before, it is important for all market participants to become familiar with the two-way relationship between the two markets. The relationship is represented by the credit default swap basis: a measure of the difference in price and value between the cash and synthetic credit markets.

The growth of the credit derivatives market has produced a highly liquid market in credit default swaps across the credit curve. This liquidity in turn has helped to generate further growth in the market. There is a wide range of users of credit default swaps, from banks and other financial institutions to corporate and supranational bodies. The liquid nature of the credit default swap market has resulted in many investors accessing synthetic, rather than cash, markets in corporate credit. As well as greater liquidity, the synthetic market also offers investors the opportunity to access any part of the credit term structure, and not just those parts of the term structure where corporate borrowers have issued bonds. The liquidity of the synthetic market has resulted in many investors accessing both the credit derivatives and the cash bond markets to meet their investment requirements.

This book considers the close relationship between the synthetic and cash markets in credit. We look first at why in theory the price of the cash and synthetic products should be identical. We then look at why the synthetic market price will necessarily differ from the cash market price. We consider the factors that drive this non–zero basis, and the implications this has for market participants. We consider the latest developments and the most effective approach to calculate the basis. We discuss the concept of the basis trade, the quintessential arbitrage trade, and the mechanics behind it. Because the basis is a quantitative measure of relative value between cash and synthetic credit markets, any calculation methodology needs to compare like-for-like yield spreads. We assess the different methodologies that may be employed, and conclude that the adjusted basis—which is the difference between the adjusted CDS spread, or C-spread, and the cash bond Z-spread—is the most effective measure of the basis. The adjusted CDS spread uses the synthetic market credit term structure to adjust cash bond market yields. Finally, we illustrate key concepts with real-world examples of positive and negative basis arbitrage trades. But to begin with, we present some essential background on the CDS itself, the concept of bond spreads and relative value, and plain vanilla CDS pricing.

An understanding of the basis is, we feel, of vital importance to anyone with an involvement in the credit-risky debt capital markets, whether as investor, trader, or broker. As such, this book is aimed at, among others, those working in financial institutions and related firms. We hope they find the content useful.

Comments on the text are welcome and should be addressed to the author care of Bloomberg Press.

Acknowledgments

Thanks to splendid chap Niall Considine at KBC Financial Products for much insight into this arcane business. Thanks also to my man Stuart Turner for review comments and assistance. Of course, any errors or omissions are the sole responsibility of the author.

Thanks to Suraj Gohil and Maj Haque at KBC FP for answering my various technical questions on CDS and the basis.

Thank you to Juan Fernández Blasco at BBVA in Madrid, an all-round top chap, for inviting me to join his panel at the ICBI derivatives conference in Paris this year.

And thanks to Tracey Parish at KBC FP. There's a picture of you in the dictionary under *reliable*.

—MOORAD CHOUDHRY
Surrey, England
June 2006

ABOUT THE AUTHOR

Moorad Choudhry is head of Treasury at KBC Financial Products in London. He is a visiting professor at the Department of Economics, London Metropolitan University; a visiting research fellow at the ICMA Centre, University of Reading; and a senior fellow at the Centre for Mathematical Trading and Finance, Cass Business School. His professional affiliations include fellow of the Institute of Sales and Marketing Management, fellow of the Global Association of Risk Professionals, and fellow of the Securities and Investment Institute. He is on the editorial board of the *Journal of Structured Finance*.

THE

CREDIT DEFAULT SWAP

BASIS

He had a faint air of the first world war about him. Just because there was a war on was no reason for lapses of courtesy, warmth, and modest behavior.

—WALTER THOMPSON
on Wing Commander Guy Gibson,
quoted in *Lancaster to Berlin*,
Goodall Publications (1985)

CHAPTER 1

A Primer on Credit Default Swaps

The basis is an important measure of relative value in credit markets. Prior to the development and introduction of credit derivatives, there was no concept of a credit basis, because there was no way to trade credit explicitly as an asset class in its own right. Credit derivatives enable such trading, and hence the emergence of a liquid market in credit derivatives has enabled investors to trade the basis across cash and synthetic (derivative) markets.

Traditionally we would define the basis as the difference between the spot price of a deliverable asset and the relative price of the shortest-duration futures contract written on the same asset. While theory would dictate that, funding or "carry" costs excepted, these two prices should be the same, in practice they are not. The real-world gaps between spot and relative price until expiry of the nearest contract mean that a non–zero basis does occur in practice. This is because of deviations created by the time gap between expiry of the futures contract and the spot commodity, differences in asset quality, location of delivery, and a number of other technical factors. Hence the basis is used by investors to gauge the profitability of delivery of cash or the actual, and they also use it to search for arbitrage opportunities. A "basis trade" is a futures trading strategy involving the purchase of a futures position to hedge against a future commitment to deliver the underlying commodity. Trading the basis is therefore putting on simultaneous positions in the cash and the derivative written on the cash. This then is the basis; the only change we make to the traditional definition is to remove the word *deliverable*, and define the basis simply as the price difference between a cash asset and the derivative or synthetic form of the same asset. The asset itself may not be a physical commodity and not necessarily deliverable.

In subsequent chapters, we provide a detailed description of the basis and the mechanics of basis trading. As important, we also suggest ways to measure the basis, which is a spread between the cash and synthetic markets. We begin, though, with a primer on credit default swaps. This is required background knowledge; more experienced practitioners can of course skip this chapter.

Credit Risk and Credit Derivatives

Credit derivatives are over-the-counter (OTC) financial contracts designed to replicate credit exposure by exhibiting a payoff profile that is linked to the occurrence of *credit events*. A payout under a credit derivative is triggered by a credit event associated with the credit derivative's *reference asset* or *reference entity*. Because financial institutions and credit rating agencies define default in different ways, the terms under which a credit derivative is executed will include a specification of what constitutes a credit event. The principle behind credit derivatives is straightforward: they enable market participants to purchase or short credit exposure synthetically, independently of whether a cash market position can be established. The flexibility of credit derivatives provides users a number of advantages, and as they are OTC products, they can be designed to meet specific user requirements.

Credit derivatives may be used to manage risk exposure inherent in a corporate or non-AAA sovereign bond portfolio, and to manage the credit risk of commercial bank loan books. Because the instruments isolate credit risk from the underlying loan or bond and transfer them to another entity, it becomes possible to separate the ownership and management of credit risk from the other features of ownership associated with the assets in question. This means that illiquid assets such as bank loans and illiquid bonds can have their credit risk exposures transferred; the bank owning the assets can protect against credit loss even if it cannot transfer the assets themselves.

For market participants, the advantages of using credit derivatives over the same reference entity's cash assets can include the following:

❑ They can be tailor-made to meet the specific requirements of the entity buying the risk protection, as opposed to the liquidity or term of the underlying reference asset.

❑ They can be "sold short" without risk of a liquidity or delivery squeeze, as it is a specific credit risk that is being traded. In the cash market, it is not possible to "sell short" a bank loan for example, but a credit derivative can be used to establish synthetically the economic effect of such a position.

❑ Because they theoretically isolate credit risk from other factors such as client relationships, funding considerations, and interest-rate risk, credit derivatives introduce a formal pricing mechanism to price credit issues only. This means a market is available in credit only, allowing more efficient pricing, and it becomes possible to model a term structure of credit rates.

❑ They are off–balance sheet instruments,[1] and as such incorporate tremendous flexibility and leverage, exactly like other financial derivatives. For instance, bank loans are not particularly attractive investments for certain investors because of the administration required in managing and servicing a loan portfolio. An exposure to bank loans and their associated return,

---

1. When credit derivatives are embedded in certain fixed income products, such as structured notes and credit-linked notes, they are then off–balance sheet, but part of a structure that will have on–balance sheet elements. Funded credit derivatives are on–balance sheet.

however, can be achieved using credit derivatives while simultaneously avoiding the administrative costs of actually owning the assets. Hence, credit derivatives allow investors access to specific credits while allowing banks access to further distribution for bank loan credit risk.

Thus, credit derivatives can be an important instrument for banks and bond portfolio managers as well as active investors such as hedge funds.

Credit Events

The occurrence of a specified credit event will trigger the termination of the credit derivative contract, and transfer of the default payment from the protection seller to the protection buyer.

The following may be specified as credit events in the legal documentation between counterparties:

- ❑ Downgrade in S&P and/or Moody's credit rating below a specified minimum level
- ❑ Financial or debt restructuring, for example occasioned under administration or as required under U.S. bankruptcy protection
- ❑ Bankruptcy or insolvency of the reference asset obligor
- ❑ Default on payment obligations such as bond coupon and continued nonpayment after a specified time period
- ❑ Technical default—for example the nonpayment of interest or coupon when it falls due
- ❑ A change in credit spread payable by the obligor above a specified maximum level

The International Swaps and Derivatives Association (ISDA) compiled standard documentation governing the legal treatment of credit derivative contracts. The standardization of legal documentation promoted ease of execution and was a factor in the rapid growth of the market. The 1999 ISDA credit default swap documentation specified bankruptcy, failure to pay, obligation default, debt moratorium, and restructuring to be credit events. Note that it does not specify a rating downgrade to be a credit event.[2]

A summary of the credit events as set forth in the ISDA definitions is given in Appendix 2.1 of Choudhry (2004).

The precise definition of *restructuring* is open to debate and has resulted in legal disputes between protection buyers and sellers. Prior to issuing its 1999 definitions, ISDA had specified restructuring as an event or events that resulted in making the terms of the reference obligation "materially less favorable" to the creditor (or protection seller) from an economic perspective. This definition is open to more than one interpretation, and caused controversy when determining if a credit event had occurred. The 2001 definitions specified more precise conditions, including any action that resulted in a reduction in the amount of principal. In the European market, restructuring is generally retained as a credit event in contract documentation, but in the U.S. market, it is less common to see restructuring included. Instead, U.S. contract documentation tends to include as a credit event a form of modified restructuring, the impact of which is to limit the options available to the protection buyer as to the type of assets he could deliver in a physically settled contract. Further clarification was provided in the 2003 ISDA definitions. For further background, see Choudhry (2004).

Credit Derivative Instruments

Before looking at the main types of credit derivative, we consider some generic details of all credit derivatives.

Introduction

Credit derivative instruments enable participants in the financial market to trade in credit as an asset, as they isolate and transfer credit risk. They also enable the market to separate funding

---

2. The ISDA definitions from 1999, the restructuring supplement from 2001, and the 2003 definitions are available at www.ISDA.org.

considerations from credit risk. A number of instruments come under the category of credit derivatives. Irrespective of the particular instrument under consideration, all credit derivatives can be described under the following characteristics:

❑ The reference entity, which is the asset or name on which credit protection is being bought and sold[3]

❑ The credit event, or events, which indicate that the reference entity is experiencing or about to experience financial difficulty, and which act as trigger events for termination of and payments under the credit derivative contract

❑ The settlement mechanism for the contract, whether cash-settled or physically settled

❑ Under physical settlement, the deliverable obligation that the protection buyer delivers to the protection seller on the occurrence of a trigger event

Funded and Unfunded Contracts

Credit derivatives are grouped into *funded* and *unfunded* instruments. In a funded credit derivative, typified by a credit-linked note (CLN), the investor in the note is the credit-protection seller and is making an up-front payment to the protection buyer when he buys the note. This up-front payment is the price of the CLN. Thus, the protection buyer is the issuer of the note. If no credit event occurs during the life of the note, the redemption value (par) of the note is paid to the investor on maturity. If a credit event does occur, then on maturity a value less than par will be paid out to the investor. This value will be reduced by the nominal value of the reference asset that the CLN is linked to. The exact process will differ according to whether *cash settlement* or *physical settlement* has been specified for the note. We will consider this later.

---

3. Note that a contract may be written in relation to a *reference entity*, which is the corporate or sovereign name, or a *reference obligation*, which is a specific debt obligation of a specific reference entity. Another term for reference obligation is *reference asset* or *reference credit*. We will use these latter terms interchangeably in the book.

In an unfunded credit derivative, typified by a credit default swap, the protection seller does not make an up-front payment to the protection buyer. Thus, the main difference between funded and unfunded is that in a funded contract, the insurance protection payment is made to the protection buyer at the start of the transaction: if there is no credit event, the payment is returned to the protection seller. In an unfunded contract, the protection payment is made on termination of the contract on occurrence of a triggering credit event. Otherwise it is not made at all. When entering into a funded contract transaction, therefore, the protection seller must find the funds at the start of the trade.

Credit default swaps have a number of applications and are used extensively for flow trading of single reference name credit risks or, in *portfolio swap form*, for trading a basket of reference obligations. Credit default swaps and CLNs are used in structured products, in various combinations, and their flexibility has been behind the growth and wide application of the synthetic collateralized debt obligation and other credit hybrid products.

Compared to cash market bonds and loans, unfunded credit derivatives isolate and transfer credit risk. In other words, their value reflects (in theory) only the credit quality of the reference entity. Compare this to a fixed-coupon corporate bond, the value of which is a function of both interest-rate risk and credit quality, and whose return to the investor will depend on the investor's funding costs.[4] The interest-rate risk element of the bond can

---

4. Funding refers to the cost of funds of the investor. For a money center bank, it will be Libid (the London interbank bid rate), although for many banks it will be between Libid and the London interbank offered rate (Libor). For a traditional investor such as a pension fund, it is more problematic, as the funds are in theory invested directly with the pension fund and so acquired "free." For economic purposes, however, such funds are valued at what rate they could be invested in the money markets. For other investors, it will be Libor plus a spread, except for very highly rated market participants, such as the World Bank, that can fund at sub-Libor.

FIGURE 1.1 *Credit derivatives isolate credit as an asset class and risk element*

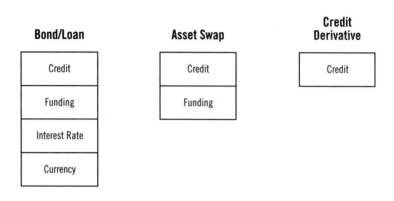

be removed by combining the bond with an interest-rate swap, to create an *asset swap*. An asset swap removes the interest-rate risk of the bond, leaving only the credit quality and the funding aspects of the bond. With an unfunded credit derivative, the funding aspect is removed as well, leaving only the credit element. This is because no up-front payment is required, resulting in no funding risk to the protection seller. The protection seller, who is the investor, receives a return that is linked only to the credit quality of the reference entity.

This separation of credit risk from other elements of the cash market is shown in **FIGURE 1.1**.

Credit Default Swaps

We describe now the credit default swap (CDS), the most commonly traded credit derivative instrument.

Structure

The most common credit derivative is the *credit default swap*, also called a *credit swap* or *default swap*. This is a bilateral con-

FIGURE 1.2 *Credit default swap*

tract that provides protection on the par value of a specified reference asset, with a protection buyer that pays a periodic fixed fee or a one-off premium to a protection seller, in return for which the seller will make a payment on the occurrence of a specified credit event. The fee is usually quoted as a basis point multiplier of the nominal value. It is usually paid quarterly in arrears. The swap can refer to a single asset, known as the reference asset or underlying asset, a basket of assets, or a reference entity. The default payment can be paid in whatever way suits the protection buyer or both counterparties. For example, it may be linked to the change in price of the reference asset or another specified asset, it may be fixed at a predetermined recovery rate, or it may be in the form of actual delivery of the reference asset at a specified price. The basic structure is illustrated in **FIGURE 1.2**.

The credit default swap enables one party to transfer its credit risk exposure to another party. Banks may use credit default swaps to trade sovereign and corporate credit spreads without trading the actual assets themselves; for example, someone who has gone long a default swap (the protection buyer) will gain if the reference asset obligor suffers a rating downgrade or defaults, and can sell the default swap at a profit if he can find a buyer counterparty.[5] This is because the cost of protection on the reference asset will have increased as a result of the credit event. The original buyer of the default swap need never have owned a bond issued by the reference asset obligor.

The maturity of the credit default swap does not have to match the maturity of the reference asset, and often does not. On occurrence of a credit event, the swap contract is terminated and a settlement payment made by the protection seller, or *guarantor*, to the protection buyer. This termination value is calculated at the time of the credit event, and the exact procedure that is followed to calculate the termination value will depend on the settlement terms specified in the contract. This will be either cash settlement or physical settlement. We look at these options later.

CDS Coupon Dates

The premiums paid on CDS contracts generally follow set standards. These standards include the following:

❑ If the trade is effected today, the effective date of the protection is tomorrow, even if tomorrow is Saturday or bank holiday; this recognizes that companies can default on a nonbusiness day.

❑ The coupon payment dates are quarterly dates, based on the maturity date of the contract. For example, if maturity is December 20, 2009, the coupon dates are going to be March 20, June 20, September 20, and December 20.

❑ The first coupon is a short one (less than 3 months) if the trade date is more than 1 month from the closest coupon date; otherwise it is a long (more than 3 months) coupon. In

---

5. Be careful with terminology here. To "go long" of an instrument generally is to purchase it. In the cash market, going long the bond means one is buying the bond and so receiving coupon; the buyer has therefore taken on credit risk exposure to the issuer. In a credit default swap, going long is to buy the swap, but the buyer is purchasing protection and therefore paying premium; the buyer has no credit exposure on the name, and has in effect "gone short" on the reference name (the equivalent of shorting a bond in the cash market and paying coupon). So buying a credit default swap is frequently referred to in the market as "shorting" the reference entity.

EXAMPLE 1.1 *Credit Default Swap*

XYZ PLC credit spreads are currently trading at 120 basis points (bps) over government for 5-year maturities, and 195 bps over for 10-year maturities. A portfolio manager hedges a $10 million holding of 10-year paper by purchasing the following credit default swap, written on the 5-year bond. This hedge protects for the first 5 years of the holding, and in the event of XYZ's credit spread widening, will increase in value and may be sold on or before expiry at profit. The 10-year bond holding also earns 75 bps over the shorter-term paper for the portfolio manager.

Term	5 years
Reference credit	XYZ PLC 5-year bond
Credit event	The business day following occurrence of specified credit event
Default payment	Nominal value of bond × [100 − price of bond after credit event]
Swap premium	3.35%

Assume now that midway into the life of the swap, there is a technical default on the XYZ PLC 5-year bond, such that its price now stands at $28. Under the terms of the swap, the protection buyer delivers the bond to the seller, who pays out $7.2 million to the buyer, as shown below:

Default payment = $10,000,000 × [100% − 28%]
= $7,200,000

our example, the first coupon is December 20, 2004. If we trade on November 20 or after, the first coupon date will be March 20, 2005.

In addition, most contracts have a "standard roll" maturity. If a bank buys "5-year protection" on December 20, 2004, it means protection to December 20, 2009. Similarly, "3-year" means "December 20, 2007." These standard maturity dates will

EXAMPLE 1.2 *Asset-Swap Terms*

Let us assume that we have a credit-risky bond with the following details:

Currency:	EUR
Issue date:	March 31, 2000
Maturity:	March 31, 2007
Coupon:	5.5% per annum
Price (dirty):	105.3%
Price (clean):	101.2%
Yield:	5%
Accrued interest:	4.1%
Rating:	A1

To buy this bond, the investor would pay 105.3% of par value. The investor would receive the fixed coupons of 5.5% of par value. Let us assume that the swap rate is 5%. The investor in this bond enters into an asset swap with a bank in which the investor pays the fixed coupon and receives Libor ± spread.

The asset-swap price (that is, spread) on this bond has the following components:

(i) the value of the excess value of the fixed coupons over the market swap rate is paid to the investor. Let us assume that in this case, this is approximately 0.5% when spread into payments over the life of the asset swap;

(ii) the difference between the bond price and par value is another factor in the pricing of an asset swap. In this case, the price premium, which is expressed in present value terms, should be spread over the term of the swap and treated as a payment by the investor to the bank (if a dirty price is at a discount to the par value, then the payment is made from the bank to the investor). For example, in this case, let us assume that this results in a payment from the investor to the bank of approximately 0.23% when spread over the term of the swap.

These two elements result in a net spread of 0.5% − 0.23% = 0.27%. Therefore, the asset swap would be quoted as Libor + 0.27% (or Libor plus 27 bps).

roll on December 20, 2004, to March 20, 2010 (respectively, March 20, 2008).

In the event of default, settlement works as follows: the protection buyer delivers a bond with his claim (excluding coupon accruals, but including premium redemption accruals) equal to the notional of the CDS, and receives notional minus accruals on the CDS since the last coupon paid. All coupons are on actual/360 basis.

We discuss settlement again later in this chapter.

Asset Swaps

Asset swaps are really interest-rate swaps that have been combined with a bond. Although they are not true credit derivatives, they are considered as being part of this market. For later analysis, we also need to know about the asset-swap spread. So we discuss them here.

Description

Asset swaps predate the introduction of the other instruments we discuss in this chapter, and strictly speaking are not credit derivatives: they are viewed as being part of the "cash market." They are used for similar purposes, however, and there is considerable interplay between the cash and synthetic markets using asset swaps; hence, we include them here. An asset swap is a combination of an interest-rate swap and a bond, and is used to alter the cash-flow profile of a bond.[6] The asset-swap market is an important segment of the credit derivatives market since it explicitly sets out the price of credit as a spread over the London interbank offered rate (Libor). Pricing a bond by reference to Libor is commonly used, and the spread over Libor is a measure of credit risk in the cash flow of the underlying bond. This is because Libor itself—the rate at which

---

6. For a background on interest-rate swaps, the reader can look up any number of sources—for instance, Das (1994), Decovny (1998), Kolb (2000), Choudhry (2001), and so on.

banks lend cash to each other in the interbank market—is viewed as representing the credit risk of banks. As such, it can be viewed as an AA or AA– credit rating. The spread over Libor therefore represents additional credit risk over and above that of bank risk.

Asset swaps are used to transform the cash-flow characteristics of a bond, either fixed rate into floating rate or floating rate into fixed rate. This enables investors to hedge the currency, credit, and interest-rate risks to create investments with more suitable cash-flow characteristics for themselves. An asset-swap package involves transactions in which the investor acquires a bond position and then enters into an interest-rate swap with the bank that sold him the bond. If it is a fixed-rate bond, the investor will pay fixed and receive floating on the interest-rate swap. This transforms the fixed coupon of the bond into a Libor-based floating coupon.

An example would be that of a protection buyer holding a fixed-rate risky bond and wishing to hedge the credit risk of this position via a credit default swap. By means of an asset swap, however, the protection seller (for example a bank) will agree to pay the protection buyer Libor ± spread in return for the cash flows of the risky bond. In this way, the protection buyer (investor) may be able to explicitly finance the credit default swap premium from the asset-swap spread income if there is a nega-

FIGURE 1.3 *Asset-swap structure*

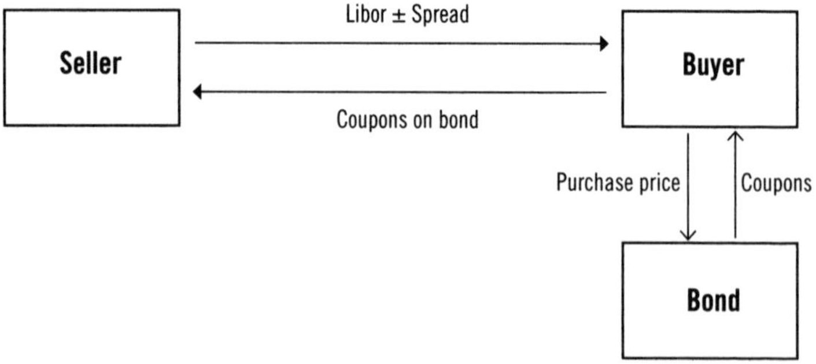

tive basis between them. If the asset swap was terminated, it is common for the buyer of the asset-swap package to take the "unwind" cost of the interest-rate swap.

FIGURE 1.3 illustrates the basic asset-swap structure.

The CDS iTraxx Index

The iTraxx series is a set of credit indexes that enable market participants to trade funded and unfunded credit derivatives linked to a credit benchmark. There are a number of different indexes covering different sectors, for example iTraxx Europe, iTraxx Japan, iTraxx Korea, and so on. The equivalent index in the North American market is known as CD-X. The iTraxx exhibits relatively high liquidity and for this reason is viewed as a credit benchmark, and its bid-offer spread is very narrow at 1–2 basis points. This contrasts with spreads generally between 10 and 30 basis points for single-name CDS contracts. Because of its liquidity and benchmark status, the iTraxx is increasingly viewed as a leading indicator of the credit market overall, and the CDS index basis is important in this regard as an indicator of relative value.

The iTraxx series is a basket of reference credits that are reviewed on a regular basis. For example, the iTraxx Europe index consists of 125 corporate reference names, so each name represents 0.8% of the basket. FIGURE 1.4 shows an extract from a Bloomberg screen for the June 2011 iTraxx Europe index, with the first page of reference names. FIGURE 1.5 shows additional terms for this index contract.[7]

The index rolls every six months (in March and September), when reference names are reviewed and the premium is set. Hence there is a rolling series of contracts with the "front contract" being the most recent. There are two standard maturities, which are 5.25 years and 10.25 years. FIGURE 1.6 shows a list of iTraxx indexes as of June 2006; the second-listed contract is the current

---

7. The screens for the iTraxx are found by typing ITRX CDS <Corp> <Go> on the BLOOMBERG PROFESSIONAL® service.

one, with a June 2011 maturity and a premium of 40 basis points
(see Figure 1.4). All existing indexes can be traded although the
most liquid index is the current one. Reference names are all investment-grade rated and are the highest traded names by CDS
volume in the past six months.

A bank buying protection in EUR 10 million notional of the
index has in effect bought protection on EUR 80,000 each of
125 single-name CDSs. The premium payable on a CDS written
on the index is set at the start of the contract and remains fixed
for its entire term; the premium is paid quarterly in arrears in the
same way as a single-name CDS. The premium remains fixed, but
of course the market value fluctuates on a daily basis. This works
as follows:

❑ The constituents of the index are set about one week before
it goes live, with the fixed premium being set two days before. The
premium is calculated as an average of all the premiums payable
on the reference names making up the index. In June 2006 the
current 5-year index for Europe was the iTraxx Europe June 2011
contract. The reference names in the index were set on March 13,
2006, with the premium fixed on March 18, 2006. The index went
live on March 20, 2006. The index is renewed every six months in
the same way.

❑ After the roll date, a trade in the iTraxx is entered into at
the current market price.

❑ Because this is different from the fixed premium, an up-
front payment is made between the protection seller and protection
buyer, which is the difference between the present values of the
fixed premium and the current market premium.

So for example, on June 21, 2006 the market price of the
June 2011 iTraxx Europe was 34 basis points. An investor selling protection on this contract would receive 40 basis points
quarterly in arrears for the five years from June 2006 to June
2011. The difference is made up front: the investor receives 40
basis points although the market level at time of trade is 34 basis
points. Therefore the protection seller pays a one-off payment of

the difference between the two values, discounted. The present value of the contract is calculated assuming a flat spread curve and a 40% recovery rate. We can use Bloomberg screen CDSW to work this out, and **FIGURE 1.7** shows such a calculation using this screen. This shows a trade for EUR 10 million notional of the current iTraxx Europe index on June 19, 2006. We see the deal spread is 40 basis points; we enter the current market price of 34 basis points and assume a flat credit term structure.

From Figure 1.7 we see that the one-off payment for this deal is EUR 27,280. The protection seller, who will receive 40 basis points quarterly in arrears for the life of the deal, pays this amount at trade inception to the protection buyer.[8]

FIGURE 1.4 *Page 1 of list of reference names in iTraxx Europe June 2011 index*

```
<HELP> for explanation.                                    P174 Corp   CDSW
1<GO> to sort by name. 3<Go> to sort by weight. 4<Go> to download to Excel.
                                                               Page 1/7
               REFERENCE ENTITY LIST
Reference Entity Legal Name              Weight (%)
ABN AMRO Bank N.V.                          0.800
ACCOR                                       0.800
Adecco S.A.                                 0.800
Aegon N.V.                                  0.800
Aktiebolaget Electrolux                     0.800
Aktiebolaget Volvo                          0.800
AKZO Nobel N.V.                             0.800
Allianz Aktiengesellschaft                  0.800
ALTADIS, S.A.                               0.800
ARCELOR FINANCE                             0.800
ASSICURAZIONI GENERALI - SOCIETA PER A      0.800
AVIVA PLC                                   0.800
AXA                                         0.800
BAA PLC                                     0.800
BAE SYSTEMS PLC                             0.800
BANCA INTESA S.P.A.                         0.800
BANCA MONTE DEI PASCHI DI SIENA S.P.A.      0.800
BANCA POPOLARE ITALIANA - BANCA POPOLA      0.800
BANCO BILBAO VIZCAYA ARGENTARIA, SOCIE      0.800
Banco Comercial Portugues, S.A.            0.800
```

8. The one-off payment reflects the difference between the prevailing market rate and the fixed rate. If the market rate was above 40 basis points at the time of this trade, the protection buyer would pay the protection seller the one-off payment reflecting this difference.

FIGURE 1.5 *Additional terms for June 2011 iTraxx Europe index*

```
<HELP> for explanation.                          P174 Corp   CDSW
<Menu> to return
```

```
┌─ ADDITIONAL  DESCRIPTIVE  INFORMATION ─┐
```

```
        Announcement Date:  0/ 0/00          Currency:    EUR
        Int. Accrual Date:  3/20/06
                                        Amt Issued:       0.00
            1st Settle Date:  3/20/06   Amt Outstanding:  0.00
            1st Coupon Date:  6/20/06
                                        Par Amount:       0.00
            Maturity Date:  6/20/11

        Payment Frequency: Q Quarterly
        Day Count Basis: ACT/360

            Business Days: EUR
        Business Day Adj: 1 Following

            Issue Spread:    40.0 bps
```

Source: Bloomberg

FIGURE 1.6 *List of iTraxx indexes as shown on the Bloomberg, June 19, 2006*

```
<HELP> for explanation, <MENU> for similar functions.    P174 Corp
```

CREDIT DEFAULT SWAPS for ticker ITRX CDS Page 1/ 11

Found   194

	ISSUER	SPREAD	MATURITY	SERS	RTNG	FREQ	TYPE	CNTRY/CURR	
1)	ITRX EUR	25	6/20/09	5EU	N.A.	Qtr	iTRAXX	EU	/EUR
2)	ITRX EUR	40	6/20/11	5EU2	N.A.	Qtr	iTRAXX	EU	/EUR
3)	ITRX EUR	50	6/20/13	5EU3	N.A.	Qtr	iTRAXX	EU	/EUR
4)	ITRX EUR	60	6/20/16	5EU4	N.A.	Qtr	iTRAXX	EU	/EUR
5)	ITRX SDI	45	6/20/16	2SD	N.A.	Qtr	iTRAXX	GB	/GBP
6)	ITRX INDS	40	6/20/11	5IND	N.A.	Qtr	iTRAXX	EU	/EUR
7)	ITRX INDS	60	6/20/16	5IN2	N.A.	Qtr	iTRAXX	EU	/EUR
8)	ITRX SUB	25	6/20/11	5SUB	N.A.	Qtr	iTRAXX	EU	/EUR
9)	ITRX SUB	45	6/20/16	5SU2	N.A.	Qtr	iTRAXX	EU	/EUR
10)	ITRX SNR FIN	15	6/20/11	5SNR	N.A.	Qtr	iTRAXX	EU	/EUR
11)	ITRX SNR FIN	25	6/20/16	5SN2	N.A.	Qtr	iTRAXX	EU	/EUR
12)	ITRX CROSS	290	6/20/11	5XOV	N.A.	Qtr	iTRAXX	EU	/EUR
13)	ITRX CROSS	350	6/20/16	5XO2	N.A.	Qtr	iTRAXX	EU	/EUR
14)	ITRX NON-FINL	40	6/20/11	5NF1	N.A.	Qtr	iTRAXX	EU	/EUR
15)	ITRX NON-FINL	60	6/20/16	5NF2	N.A.	Qtr	iTRAXX	EU	/EUR
16)	ITRX TMT	40	6/20/11	5TMT	N.A.	Qtr	iTRAXX	EU	/EUR
17)	ITRX TMT	60	6/20/16	5TM2	N.A.	Qtr	iTRAXX	EU	/EUR
18)	ITRX HVOL	40	6/20/09	5HI	N.A.	Qtr	iTRAXX	EU	/EUR
19)	ITRX HVOL	70	6/20/11	5HI2	N.A.	Qtr	iTRAXX	EU	/EUR

Source: Bloomberg

FIGURE 1.7 *Screen CDSW used to calculate up-front present value payment for trade in EUR 10 million notional iTraxx Europe index CDS contract, June 19, 2006*

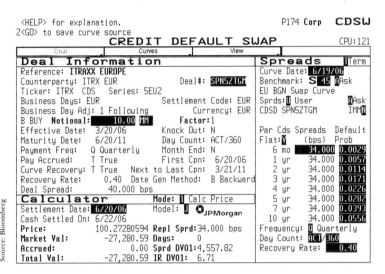

If a credit event occurs on one of the reference entities in the iTraxx, the contract is physically settled, for that name, for 0.8% of the notional value of the contract. This is similar to the way that a single-name CDS would be settled. Unlike a single-name CDS, the contract continues to maturity at a reduced notional amount. Note that European iTraxx indexes trade under Modified-Modified restructuring (MMR) terms, which is prevalent in the European market. Under MMR, a debt restructuring is named as a credit event.[9]

9. This contrasts with the North American market, which includes the CDX family of indexes, where CDSs trade under no-restructuring terms; this describes only bankruptcy and liquidation as credit events.

FIGURE 1.8A *"Telecoms & Electronics" sector CDS prices page from BBVA, March 13, 2006*

14										P1P122 **Govt** **BBCS**		
200<Go> to view in Launchpad												
10:46 **Telecoms & Electronics**										PAGE 1 / 10		
Telecoms &	Ratings		1 Year		3 Year		5 Year		5Y	10 Year		
Electonics	Mdys	S&P	Bid	Ask	Bid	Ask	Bid	Ask	Chg	Bid	Ask	Time
BRITISH TEL	Baa1	A-	9	15	25	35	47	53	--	82	92	2/27
DEUTSCHE TEL	A3	A-	8	14	24	34	45	51	-2	82	92	2/27
ELECTROLUX	Baa1	BBB+	14	20	31	41	53	63	+3	84	94	2/27
FRANCE TELECOM	A3	A-	9	15	26	36	47	53	-2	86	96	2/27
KPN	Baa2	BBB+	18	24	51	61	90	96	+9	132	142	2/27
MMO2	Baa2	BBB+	6	12	18	28	34	40	-2	57	67	2/27
NOKIA				6	5	15	12	22	--	31	41	2/27
OTE	A3	BBB+	12	18	30	40	53	59	+2	222	232	2/27
PHILIPS	Baa1	A-	3	9	12	22	21	31	--	44	54	2/27
PORTUGAL TEL	Baa1	BBB+	-2	4	99	109	170	176	+43	222	232	2/27
SIEMENS	Aa3	N.A.	3	9	7	17	16	26	--	34	44	2/27
STM	N.A.	NR	3	9	9	19	18	28	+2	36	46	2/27

Tel: +34 91 537 6087
INDICATIVE PRICES FOR CREDIT DEFAULT SWAPS ON STANDARD
ISDA 2003 DOCUMENTATION WITH 3 CREDIT EVENTS
MATURITIES ARE ON QUARTERLY BASIS   **BBVA**

FIGURE 1.8B *"Autos" sector CDS prices page from BBVA, March 13, 2006*

04										P1P122		
200<Go> to view in Launchpad												
10:46 **Autos**										PAGE 1 / 10		
	Ratings		1 Year		3 Year		5 Year		5Y	10 Year		
Autos	Mdys	S&P	Bid	Ask	Bid	Ask	Bid	Ask	Chg	Bid	Ask	Time
BMW	A1	N.A.	4	10	12	18	22	24	--	38	48	2/27
CONTINENTAL	Baa1	BBB+	9	15	18	24	45	49	-2	71	81	2/27
DCX	A3	BBB	13	19	25	31	62	65	-3	91	101	2/27
FIAT	Ba3	N.A.	15	75	75	135	233	293	-18	311	371	2/27
FORD MC	Ba2	BB-	332	362	471	501	500	530	+14	499	529	2/27
GMAC	Ba1	BB	474	504	483	513	460	490	+33	451	481	2/27
MICHELIN	Baa1	BBB+	7	13	16	22	35	39	-1	54	64	2/27
PEUGEOT	WR	NR	5	11	12	18	31	35	--	51	61	2/27
RENAULT	Baa1	BBB+	7	13	15	21	36	39	-1	56	66	2/27
ROBERT BOSCH	N.A.	AA-	1	7	11	17	12	18	-1	20	30	2/27
SCANIA	N.A.	A-	4	10	15	21	38	42	+3	53	63	2/27
TOYOTA	WR	NR					6	10	-1	7	17	2/27

Tel: +34 91 537 6087
INDICATIVE PRICES FOR CREDIT DEFAULT SWAPS ON STANDARD
ISDA 2003 DOCUMENTATION WITH 3 CREDIT EVENTS
MATURITIES ARE ON QUARTERLY BASIS   **BBVA**

CDS Price Quotes

The BLOOMBERG PROFESSIONAL® service provides a number of pages for CDS and asset-swap analytics, some of which will be used to illustrate techniques in this book, as well as contributed pages for CDS prices.

Market prices are supplied by a number of investment banks. Most banks make their price screens available only to clients, or on request. Banco Bilbao Vizcaya Argentaria (BBVA) is a market maker whose screen is available to all users. Its screens of CDS prices for the "Telecoms & Electronics" and "Autos" sectors are shown in **FIGURES 1.8A** and **1.8B**, respectively; these screens show indicative quotes for 1-, 3-, 5-, and 10-year CDS contracts, both bid and offer, together with the change from the last quote.

Settlement

Credit derivative settlement can follow one of two routes, specified at deal inception. With all credit derivatives, upon occurrence of a credit event, a credit event notice must be submitted. Typically, the notice must be supported by information posted on public news systems such as Bloomberg or Reuters. When used as part of a structured product, the terms of the deal may state that a credit event must be verified by a third-party *verification agent*. Upon verification, the contract will be settled in one of two ways: cash settlement or physical settlement.

A report from the British Bankers' Association (BBA) suggested that 75% to 85% of credit derivatives written in 2002 were physically settled, while about 10% to 20% were cash-settled. About 5% of contracts were settled under the *fixed amount* approach, under which the protection seller delivers a prespecified amount to the protection buyer ahead of the determination of the reference asset's recovery value. Because the fixed amount approach is essentially cash settlement, however, we will consider it as such and prefer the more technical term for it noted below.

Contract Settlement Options

Credit derivatives have a given maturity, but will terminate early if a credit event occurs. On occurrence of a credit event, the swap contract is terminated and a settlement payment made by the protection seller, or guarantor, to the protection buyer. This termination value is calculated at the time of the credit event, and the procedure that is followed to calculate the termination value will depend on the settlement terms specified in the contract. Credit derivatives specify physical or cash settlement. In physical settlement, the protection buyer transfers to the protection seller the deliverable obligation (usually the reference asset or assets), with the total principal outstanding equal to the nominal specified in the default swap contract. The protection seller simultaneously pays to the buyer 100% of the nominal. In cash settlement, the protection seller hands to the buyer the difference between the nominal amount of the default swap and the final value for the same nominal amount of the reference asset. This final value is usually determined by means of a poll of dealer banks. This final value is in theory the recovery value of the asset; because the recovery process can take some time, however, often the reference asset market value at time of default is taken, and this amount used in calculating the final settlement amount paid to the protection buyer.

The settlement mechanisms are shown in **FIGURE 1.9**, and follow the following process:

❏ *Cash settlement:* the contract may specify a predetermined payout value on occurrence of a credit event. This may be the nominal value of the swap contract. Such a swap is known as a *fixed amount* contract or, in some markets, as a *digital credit derivative.* Alternatively, the termination payment is calculated as the difference between the nominal value of the reference asset and either its market value at the time of the credit event or its recovery value. This arrangement is more common with cash-settled contracts.[10]

---

10. Determining the market value of the reference asset at the time of the credit event may be a little problematic: the issuer of the asset may well be in default or administration. An independent third-party *calculation agent* is usually employed to make the termination payment calculation.

FIGURE 1.9 *Cash and physical settlement*

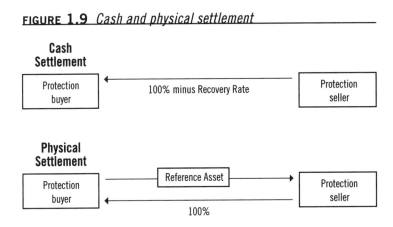

□ *Physical settlement:* on occurrence of a credit event, the buyer delivers the reference asset to the seller, in return for which the seller pays the face value of the delivered asset to the buyer. The contract may specify a number of alternative assets that the buyer can deliver; these are known as *deliverable obligations*. This may apply when a swap has been entered into on a reference name rather than a specific obligation (such as a particular bond) issued by that name. Where more than one deliverable obligation is specified, the protection buyer will invariably deliver the asset that is the cheapest on the list of eligible assets. This gives rise to the concept of the *cheapest-to-deliver*, as encountered with government bond futures contracts, and is in effect an embedded option afforded the protection buyer.

In theory, the value of protection is identical irrespective of which settlement option is selected. Under physical settlement, however, the protection seller can gain if there is a recovery value that can be extracted from the defaulted asset; or its value may rise as the fortunes of the issuer improve.

Swap market-making banks often prefer cash settlement, as there is less administration associated with it, since there is no delivery of a physical asset. For a CDS used as part of a structured product, cash settlement may be more suitable because such vehicles may not be set up to take delivery of physical assets. Another advantage of cash settlement is that it does not expose the protection buyer to any risks should there not be any deliverable assets in the market, for instance due to shortage of liquidity in the market—were this to happen, the buyer may find the value of his settlement payment reduced. Nevertheless, physical settlement is widely used because counterparties wish to avoid the difficulties associated with determining the market value of the reference asset under cash settlement.[11] Physical settlement also permits protection sellers to take part in the creditor negotiations with the reference entity's administrators, which may result in improved terms for them as holders of the asset.

Cash settlement is sometimes proceeded with even for physically settled contracts when, for one reason or another, it is not possible to deliver a physical asset—for instance if none is available.

Market Requirements

Various market participants have different requirements, and so may have their own preferences with regard to the settlement mechanism. A protection seller may prefer physical settlement for particular reference assets if he believes that a higher recovery value for the asset can be gained by holding on to it and/or entering into the administration process. A protection buyer may have different interests. For instance, unless the protection buyer already holds the deliverable asset (in which case the transaction he has

---

11. Credit derivative market makers may value two instruments written on the same reference entity, and with all other terms and conditions identical except that one is cash-settled and the other physically settled, at the same price. This is because, although the protection buyer has a delivery option and will deliver the cheapest bond available—an option that carries value—in a cash-settled contract, the protection buyer will nominate this same bond to be used in the calculation of the settlement of the contract. So the value of the delivery option may not result in a higher price quote from a market maker for a physically delivered contract.

entered into is a classic hedge for an asset already owned), he may prefer cash settlement, if he has a negative view of the reference obligation and has used the CDS or other credit derivative to create a synthetic short bond position. Or the protection buyer may prefer physical settlement because he views the delivery option as carrying some value.

CDS Valuation

We consider now two approaches to pricing a CDS contract, both of which are used in the market. The first we describe is termed the "reduced form" model, developed by Hull and White (2000). The second is a market approach first described by JPMorgan, which extracts a default term structure from bond market prices and is straightforward to apply in practice.

FIGURE 1.10 *Illustration of cash flows in a default swap*

a) no default

b) default

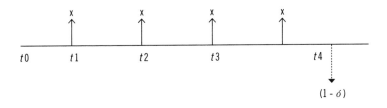

Pricing Methodology Based on Reduced-Form Model Approach[12]

A credit default swap, like an interest-rate swap, consists of two legs—one corresponding to the premium payments, and the other to the contingent default payment. This is illustrated in **FIGURE 1.10**. The present value (PV) of a default swap can be viewed as the algebraic sum of the present values of its two legs. The market premium is similar to an interest-rate swap in that the premium makes the current aggregate PV equal to zero.

The CDS is priced on the assumption that there is a recovery amount that is a fraction of the recovery rate R of par value, plus any accrued interest.

Because these cash flows may terminate at an unknown time during the life of the deal, their values are computed in a probabilistic sense, using the discounted expected value as calculated under the risk-neutral method and assumptions.

The theoretical pricing of credit derivatives has attracted attention in the academic literature. Longstaff and Schwartz (1995) present the pricing of credit spread options based on exogenous mean-reverting process for credit spreads. Duffie (1999) presents a simple argumentation for the replication of, as well as a simple reduced-form model of, the instrument. Here, we introduce a reduced-form type pricing model developed by Hull and White (2000). Their approach was to calibrate their model based on the traded bonds of the underlying reference name on a time series of credit default swap prices.

Like most other approaches, their model assumes that there is no counterparty default risk. Default probabilities, interest rates, and recovery rates are independent.

Finally, Hull and White also assume that the claim in the event of default is the face value plus accrued interest. To illustrate, we consider the valuation of a plain vanilla credit default swap with $1 notional principal.

---

12. This section was coauthored with Abukar Ali.

We use the following notation:

T is life of credit default swap in years

$q(t)$ is risk-neutral probability density at time t

R is expected recovery rate on the reference obligation in a risk-neutral world (independent of the time of default)

$u(t)$ is present value of payments at the rate of $1 per year on payment dates between time zero and time t

$e(t)$ is present value of an accrual payment at time t equal to $t - t^*$ where t^* is the payment date immediately preceding time t

$v(t)$ is present value of $1 received at time t

w is total payment per year made by credit default swap buyer

s is value of w that causes the value of credit default swap to have a value of zero

π is the risk-neutral probability of no credit event during the life of the swap

$A(t)$ is accrued interest on the reference obligation at time t as a percentage of face value

The value π is one minus the probability that a credit event will occur by time T. This is also referred to as the survival probability, and can be calculated from $q(t)$ as follows:

$$\pi = 1 - \int_0^T q(t)dt. \qquad (1.1)$$

The payments last until a credit event or until time T, whichever is sooner. If default occurs at $t(t<T)$, the present value of the payment is $w[u(t)]$. If there is no default prior to time T, the present value of the payment is $wu(T)$. The expected present value of the payment is therefore

$$w\int_0^T q(t)[u(t) + e(t)]dt + w\pi u(T). \qquad (1.2)$$

Given the assumption about the claim amount, the risk-neutral expected payoff from the CDS contract is derived as follows:

$$1 - R[1 + A(t)] \text{ multiplying } -R \text{ by } [1 + A(t)]$$
$$1 - R[1 + A(t)] = 1 - R - A(t)R.$$

The present value of the expected payoff from the CDS is given as

$$\int_0^T [1 - R - A(t)R]q(t)v(t)dt. \qquad (1.3)$$

The value of the CDS to the buyer is the present value of the expected payoff minus the present value of the payments made by the buyer, or

$$\int_0^T [1 - R - A(t)R]q(t)v(t)dt - w\int_0^T q(t)[u(t) + e(t)]dt + w\pi u(T). \quad (1.4)$$

In equilibrium, the present value of each leg of the above equation should be equal. We can now calculate the credit default swap spread s, which is the value of w that makes the equation equal to zero, by simply rearranging the equation, as shown below.

$$s = \frac{\int_0^T [1 - R - A(t)R]q(t)v(t)dt}{\int_0^T q(t)[u(t) + e(t)]dt + \pi u(T)} \qquad (1.5)$$

The variable s is referred to as the CDS spread.

The formula at equation (1.5) is simple and intuitive for developing an analytical approach for pricing credit default swaps because of the assumptions used. For example, the model assumes that interest rates and default events are independent; also, the possibility of counterparty default is ignored. The spread s is the payment per year, as a percentage of notional principal, for a newly issued credit default swap.

FIGURE 1.11 shows the CDSW page on the Bloomberg using

FIGURE 1.11   *Bloomberg page CDSW using modified Hull-White pricing for selected credit default swap, April 12, 2006*

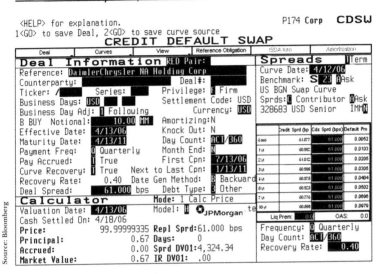

Source: Bloomberg

the modified Hull and White model.[13] Certain default parameter inputs (for the DaimlerChrysler 5-year CDS) are selected. This implementation links the rates observed in the credit-protection market and the corporate bond market, via probabilities of default of the issuer. The input used to price the CDS contract is selected from a range of market-observed yield curves, and can include:

❑ A curve of CDS spreads

❑ An issuer (credit-risky) par yield curve

❑ A default probability curve (derived from the default probabilities of the underlying reference for each maturity implied by the par credit default swap spreads)

The assumptions based on the independence of recovery rates,

---

13. A description of this page is given in Appendix I.

default probabilities, and interest rates may not hold completely in practice, since high interest rates may cause companies to experience default or administration. As a result, default probabilities would increase. Hence, a positive relation between interest rates and default probabilities may be associated with high discount rates for the CDS payoffs. This would have the effect of reducing the credit default swap spread. Nevertheless, the modified Hull-White approach presents a neat and intuitive approach that allows for a closed-form pricing approach for credit default swaps, using parameter inputs from the market.

Market Pricing Approach [14]

We now present a discrete form pricing approach that is used in the market, using market-observed parameter inputs.

We stated earlier that a CDS has two cash-flow legs; the fee premium leg and the contingent cash-flow leg. We wish to determine the par spread, or premium, of the CDS, remembering that for a par spread valuation, in accordance with no-arbitrage principles, the net present value of both legs must be equal to zero (that is, they have the same valuation).

The valuation of the fee leg is given by the following relationship:

$$PV \text{ of No-default fee payments} = s_N \times \text{Annuity}_N,$$

which is given by

$$PV = s_N \sum_{i=1}^{N} DF_i.PND_i.A_i, \qquad (1.6)$$

where

s_N is the par spread (CDS premium) for maturity N
DF_i is the risk-free discount factor from time T_0 to time T_i
PND_i is the no-default probability from T_0 to T_i
A_i is the accrual period from T_i-1 to T_i.

---

14. A more descriptive explanation of this approach, including Excel spreadsheet formulas, is given in Appendix II.

Note that the value for PND is for the specific reference entity for which a CDS is being priced.

If the accrual fee for the CDS is paid upon default and termination,[15] then the valuation of the fee leg is given by the following relationship:

PV of no-default fee payments $+$ PV of default accruals

$= s_N \times Annuity_N + s_N \times DefaultAccrual_N$

which is given by

$$PV_{NoDefault+DefaultAccrual} = s_N \sum_{i=1}^{N} DF_i.PND_i.A_i$$

$$+ s_N \sum_{i=1}^{N} DF_i.\left(PND_{i-1} - PND_i\right).\frac{A_i}{2}, \qquad (1.7)$$

where

$(PND_{i-1} - PND_i)$ is the probability of a credit event occurring during the period T_{i-1} to T_i

$\dfrac{A_i}{2}$ is the average accrual amount from T_{i-1} to T_i.

The valuation of the contingent leg is approximated by

$$PV \text{ of Contingent } = \text{ Contingent}_N,$$

which is given by

$$PV_{Contingent} = \left(1-R\right) \sum_{i=1}^{N} DF_i.\left(PND_{i-1} - PND_i\right), \qquad (1.8)$$

where R is the recovery rate of the reference obligation.

---

15. This is the amount of premium payable from the last payment date up to termination date, and similar to accrued coupon on a cash bond. Upon occurrence of a credit event and termination, the accrued premium to date is payable immediately. No protection payment is due from the protection seller until and after the accrual payment is made.

For a par credit default swap, we know that

Valuation of leg fee = Valuation of contingent leg,

and therefore we can set

$$s_N \sum_{i=1}^{N} DF_i.PND_i.A_i + s_N \sum_{i=1}^{N} DF_i.\left(PND_{i-1} - PND_i\right).\frac{A_i}{2}$$

$$= \left(1 - R\right) \sum_{i=1}^{N} DF_i.\left(PND_{i-1} - PND_i\right) \qquad (1.9)$$

TABLE 1.1 _Example of CDS spread pricing_

MATURITY t	SPOT RATES	DISCOUNT FACTORS DFj	SURVIVAL PROBABILITY PSj	DEFAULT PROBABILITY PDj
0.5	3.57%	0.9826	0.9993	0.0007
1.0	3.70%	0.9643	0.9983	0.0017
1.5	3.81%	0.9455	0.9972	0.0028
2.0	3.95%	0.9254	0.9957	0.0043
2.5	4.06%	0.9053	0.9943	0.0057
3.0	4.16%	0.8849	0.9932	0.0068
3.5	4.24%	0.8647	0.9900	0.0100
4.0	4.33%	0.8440	0.9886	0.0114
4.5	4.42%	0.8231	0.9859	0.0141
5.0	4.45%	0.8044	0.9844	0.0156

RECOVERY RATE

0.3

which may be rearranged to give us the formula for the CDS
premium s as follows:

$$s_N = (1-R) \sum_{i=1}^{N} \frac{DF_i.(PND_{i-1} - PND_i)}{\sum_{i=1}^{N} DF_i.PND_i.A_i + DF_i.(PND_{i-1} - PND_i).\frac{A_i}{2}}.$$

(1.10)

In **TABLE 1.1**, we illustrate an application of the expression in
equation (1.10) for a CDS of varying maturities, assuming a recovery rate of the defaulted reference asset of 30% and a given

	PROBABILITY-WEIGHTED PVs		
PV OF RECEIPTS IF NO DEFAULT	PV OF RECEIPTS IF DEFAULT	DEFAULT PAYMENT IF DEFAULT	CDS PREMIUM s
0.4910	0.0002	0.0005	0.10%
0.9723	0.0006	0.0016	0.17%
1.4437	0.0012	0.0035	0.24%
1.9044	0.0022	0.0063	0.33%
2.3545	0.0035	0.0099	0.42%
2.7939	0.0050	0.0141	0.50%
3.2220	0.0072	0.0201	0.62%
3.6392	0.0096	0.0269	0.74%
4.0450	0.0125	0.0350	0.86%
4.4409	0.0156	0.0438	0.98%

term structure of interest rates. It uses actual/360-day count convention.

For readers' reference, we present a fuller explanation of this valuation approach in Appendix II.

We can use CDS prices to extract a market-implied timing of default. Given that the CDS has a specified fixed term to maturity, it is possible by applying break-even analysis to extract a market-implied timing of default for the reference credit in question. This is done by calculating the amount of time that has to elapse before the premium income on the CDS equals the recovery value. By definition therefore, we require an assumed recovery rate to perform this calculation. An illustration of this process is given in Appendix III.

References

Choudhry, M. 2001. *The bond and money markets: Strategy, trading, analysis.* Oxford: Butterworth-Heinemann.

———. 2003. Some issues in the asset-swap pricing of credit default swaps. In *Professional perspectives on fixed income portfolio management,* vol. 4, ed. F. Fabozzi. Hoboken, NJ: John Wiley & Sons.

———. 2004. *Structured credit products: Credit derivatives and synthetic securitisation.* Singapore: John Wiley & Sons.

Das, S. 1994. *Swaps and financial derivatives.* London: IFR Publishing.

Decovny, S. 1998. *Swaps,* 2nd ed. Upper Saddle River, NJ: Prentice Hall.

Duffie, D. 1999. Credit swap valuation. *Financial Analysts Journal* (January–February): 73–87.

Duffie, D., and M. Huang. 1996. Swap rates and credit quality. *Journal of Finance* 51 (3): 921–49.

Francis, J., J. Frost, and J. Whittaker. 1999. *The handbook of credit derivatives.* New York: McGraw-Hill.

Hull, J., and A. White. 2000. Valuing credit default swaps I: No counterparty default risk. *Journal of Derivatives* 8 (1) (Fall): 29–40.

Jarrow, R.A., and S.M. Turnbull. 1995. Pricing options on derivative securities subject to credit risk. *Journal of Finance* 50 (1): 53–58.

Kolb, Robert W. 2000. *Futures, options and swaps*, 3rd ed. Oxford: Black-well.

Longstaff, F.A., and E.S. Schwartz. 1995. Valuing credit derivatives. *Journal of Fixed Income* 5 (1): 6–12.

CHAPTER 2

Bond Spreads and Relative Value

The credit default swap (CDS) basis is an important measure of relative value in the credit markets. Before considering the basis itself, we must familiarize ourselves with some basic concepts of bond spreads. An understanding of these is important when we consider the CDS basis later. In this chapter, we also introduce the theoretical concept of the cash market–synthetic market basis, when we consider (and then discard) the asset-swap pricing methodology for CDS contracts.

Bond Spreads

Investors measure the perceived market value, or relative value, of a corporate bond by measuring its yield spread relative to a designated benchmark. This is the spread over the benchmark that gives the yield of the corporate bond. A key measure of relative value of a corporate bond is its swap spread. This is the basis-point spread over the interest-rate swap curve, and is a measure of the credit risk of the bond. In its simplest form, the swap spread can be measured as the difference between the yield-to-maturity of the bond and the interest rate given by a straight-line interpolation of the swap curve. In practice, traders use the asset-swap spread and the Z-spread as the main measures of relative value.

The government bond spread is also used. In addition, now that the market in synthetic corporate credit is well established, using credit derivatives and CDS, investors consider the cash-CDS spread as well, which is the *basis*, and which we consider in greater detail later.

The spread that is selected is an indication of the relative value of the bond, and a measure of its credit risk. The greater the perceived risk, the greater the spread should be. This is best illustrated by the credit structure of interest rates, which will (generally) show AAA- and AA-rated bonds trading at the lowest spreads, and BBB-, BB-, and lower-rated bonds trading at the highest spreads. Bond spreads are the most commonly used indication of the risk-return profile of a bond.

In this section, we consider the Treasury spread, asset-swap spread, Z-spread and basis.

Swap Spread and Treasury Spread

A bond's swap spread is a measure of the credit risk of that bond, relative to the interest-rate swaps market. Because the swaps market is traded by banks, this risk is effectively the interbank market, so the credit risk of the bond over and above bank risk is given by its spread over swaps. This is a simple calculation to make, and is simply the yield of the bond minus the swap rate for the appropriate maturity swap. **FIGURE 2.1** shows Bloomberg page IRSB for pounds sterling as of September 22, 2005. This shows the GBP swap curve on the left-hand side. The right-hand side of the screen shows the swap rates' spread over U.K. gilts. It is the spread over these swap rates that would provide the simplest relative value measure for corporate bonds denominated in GBP. If the bond has an odd maturity, say 5.5 years, we would interpolate between the 5-year and 6-year swap rates.

The spread over swaps is sometimes called the *I-spread*. It has a simple relationship to swaps and Treasury yields, shown here in the equation for corporate bond yield

$$Y = I + S + T, \tag{2.1}$$

FIGURE 2.1 *Bloomberg page IRSB for pounds sterling, showing GBP swap rates and swap spread over U.K. gilts, September 22, 2005*

GRAB　　　　　　　　　　　　　　　　　　　　　　　　Govt　**IRSB**

British Pound

GBP Swap Rates

Ticker	TIME	Bid	Ask	Change	Open	High	Low	Prev Cls
2) 1 YR	11:22	4.4940	4.5020	--	4.4980	4.5005	4.4870	4.4990
3) 18 MO	11:22	4.3925	4.4225	-.0067	4.4150	4.4175	4.3950	4.4183
4) 2 YR	11:18	4.4070	4.4150	-.0055	4.4150	4.4225	4.3975	4.4175
5) 3 YR	11:23	4.4110	4.4350	-.0008	4.4225	4.4275	4.4000	4.4238
6) 4 YR	11:23	4.4150	4.4150	-.0118	4.4250	4.4615	4.4085	4.4263
7) 5 YR	11:23	4.4230	4.4240	-.0127	4.4350	4.4370	4.4125	4.4363
8) 6 YR	11:23	4.4340	4.4625	-.0030	4.4500	4.4550	4.4233	4.4513
9) 7 YR	11:23	4.4440	4.4620	-.0157	4.4600	4.4690	4.4395	4.4638
10) 8 YR	11:23	4.4620	4.4590	-.0150	4.4675	4.4750	4.4422	4.4713
11) 9 YR	11:23	4.4580	4.4630	-.0157	4.4725	4.4800	4.4478	4.4783
12) 10 YR	11:23	4.4610	4.4640	-.0136	4.4750	4.4840	4.4650	4.4763
13) 12 YR	11:23	4.4610	4.4640	-.0138	4.4750	4.4850	4.4585	4.4763
14) 15 YR	11:23	4.4520	4.4650	-.0128	4.4650	4.4735	4.4335	4.4663
15) 20 YR	11:23	4.4210	4.4230	-.0119	4.4325	4.5250	4.3912	4.4338
16) 25 YR	11:21	4.3175	4.4475	-.0126	4.3975	4.4367	4.3763	4.3983
17) 30 YR	11:21	4.3430	4.3550	-.0078	4.3550	4.4600	4.3225	4.3588

GBP Swap Spread

Ticker	TIME	Bid	Ask	Change	Open	High	Low	Prev Cls
19) 1 YR	11:22	33.80	39.80	+2.10	31.40	33.80	29.90	31.7000
20) 2 YR	11:21	29.50	33.50	+1.00	29.00	32.25	28.50	30.5000
21) 3 YR	11:21	31.00	35.00	+.75	30.75	33.25	30.00	32.2500
22) 4 YR	11:23	30.50	35.50	+.50	30.50	33.25	30.00	32.5000
23) 5 YR	11:14	26.50	36.00	-4.50	30.50	30.50	28.50	33.0000
24) 6 YR	11:23	32.75	37.75	+.50	32.50	35.50	32.50	34.7500
25) 7 YR	11:23	32.00	37.00	+.50	32.00	34.75	32.00	34.0000
26) 8 YR	11:21	31.00	36.00	+.50	30.75	33.75	30.75	33.0000
27) 9 YR	11:21	29.75	34.75	+.50	29.75	32.50	29.75	31.7500
28) 10 YR	8:05	29.75	34.75	+.25	32.25	32.50	32.25	32.0000
29) 15 YR	11:21	22.75	31.75	+.25	27.25	28.00	27.00	27.0000
30) 20 YR	11:21	19.00	32.00	+.13	25.50	26.00	25.25	25.3750
31) 30 YR	11:23	14.75	27.50	+.25	21.00	21.50	20.63	20.8750

For UK Govt Yield Curve, Click on any Tickers above & Select: IYC1 I22
For GBP Swap Curve, Click on any Tickers above & Select: IYC1 I55

Page 1　　　　　　　　　　　　　　　　　　　　Page 2

where

Y　is the yield on the corporate bond

I　is the I-spread, or spread over swap

S　is the swap spread

T　is the yield on the Treasury security (or an interpolated yield).

In other words, the swap rate itself is given by $T + S$.

The I-spread is sometimes used to compare a cash bond with its equivalent CDS price, but for straightforward relative value analysis, is usually dropped in favor of the asset-swap spread, which we look at later in this section.

Of course the basic relative value measure is the Treasury spread, or government bond spread. This is simply the spread of the bond yield over the yield of the appropriate government bond. Again, an interpolated yield may need to be used to obtain the right Treasury rate to use. The bond spread is given by

$$BS = Y - T.$$

Using an interpolated yield is not strictly accurate because yield curves are smooth in shape, and so straight-line interpolation will produce slight errors. The method is still commonly used, though.

Asset-Swap Spread

An asset swap is a package that combines an interest-rate swap with a cash bond, the effect of the combined package being to transform the interest-rate basis of the bond. Typically, a fixed-rate bond will be combined with an interest-rate swap in which the bondholder pays fixed coupon and receives floating coupon. The floating coupon will be a spread over Libor (see Choudhry et al. [2001]). This spread is the asset-swap spread, and is a function of the credit risk of the bond over and above interbank credit risk.[1] Asset swaps may be transacted at par or at the bond's market price, usually par. This means that the asset-swap value is made up of the difference between the bond's market price and par, as well as the difference between the bond coupon and the swap fixed rate.

The zero-coupon curve is used in the asset-swap valuation. This curve is derived from the swap curve, so it is the implied zero-coupon curve. The asset-swap spread is the spread that equates the difference between the present value of the bond's cash flows, calculated using the swap zero rates, and the market price of the bond. This spread is a function of the bond's market price and yield, its cash flows, and the implied zero-coupon interest rates.[2]

---

1. This is because in the interbank market, two banks transacting an interest-rate swap will be paying/receiving the fixed rate and receiving/paying Libor-flat. See also the author's "Learning Curve" article on asset swaps, available at www .yieldcurve.com.

2. Bloomberg refers to this spread as the gross spread.

FIGURE 2.2 *Bloomberg page ASW for GKN bond, August 10, 2005*

GRAB   Corp **ASW**

ASSET SWAP CALCULATOR   Page 1 of 3
GKN HOLDINGS PLC GKNLN 7 05/14/12   105.1200/105.6800 (6.05/5.95) BGN @16:00

Currency	Bond	Underlying Curves
From GBP To GBP	Buy/Sell S Par Amt 1000 M	Price Date BP BP
	Workout 5/14/12 @ 100.0000	8/10/05 22<SWDF#> 22
	Swap	Crv Settle B/A/M
Spot F/X 1.000	Coupon Day Count Freq	8/15/05 BGN BGN
	Fixed 4.76384% ACT/ACT 1	Z-Spread
Trade Settlement	Floating 4.64635% ACT/365 2	118.8 bp
8/15/05	Swap Par Amt(FLT) 1000 M	

Gross Spread Valuation

	Money	Spread(bp)
Implied Value 112.6477	69.7M =	**121.5**

Swapped Spread Details

Calculate 3		Money	Spread(bp)
1:Bond Price 105.6800/ 5.94627%			
Swap Price 100 Cash Out 5.6800		-56.8M =	-99.1 bp
2:Swap Rate 4.76384% Bond Cpn 7.0000		126.5M =	220.6
Redemption Premium / Discount 0.0000%		0.0 =	0.0
Funding Spread 0.0 bp		0.0M =	0.0
3:Swapped Spread			**121.5** bp

1 <Go> for X-currency spread summary, 2 <Go> to save, 3 <Go> to update swap crv

FIGURE 2.2 shows the Bloomberg screen ASW for a GBP-denominated bond, GKN Holdings 7% 2012, as of August 10, 2005. We see that the asset-swap spread is 121.5 basis points. This is the spread over Libor that will be received if the bond is purchased in an asset-swap package. In essence, the asset-swap spread measures a difference between the market price of the bond and the value of the bond when cash flows have been valued using zero-coupon rates. The asset-swap spread can therefore be regarded as the coupon of an annuity in the swap market that equals this difference.

Z-Spread

The conventional approach for analyzing an asset swap uses the bond's yield-to-maturity (YTM) in calculating the spread. The assumptions implicit in the YTM calculation (see Chapter 6 of Choudhry et al. [2001]) make this spread problematic for relative analysis, so market practitioners use what is termed the Z-spread instead. The Z-spread uses the zero-coupon yield curve to cal-culate spread, so is a more realistic, and effective, spread to use. The zero-coupon curve used in the calculation is derived from the interest-rate swap curve.

Put simply, the Z-spread is the basis-point spread that would need to be added to the implied spot yield curve such that the discounted cash flows of a bond are equal to its present value (its current market price). Each bond cash flow is discounted by the relevant spot rate for its maturity term. How does this differ from the conventional asset-swap spread? Essentially, in its use of zero-coupon rates when assigning a value to a bond. Each cash flow is discounted using its own particular zero-coupon rate. The price of a bond at any time can be taken to be the market's value of the bond's cash flows. Using the Z-spread, we can quantify what the swap market thinks of this value—that is, by how much the conventional spread differs from the Z-spread. Both spreads can be viewed as the coupon of a swap market annuity of equivalent credit risk of the bond being valued.

In practice, the Z-spread, especially for shorter-dated bonds and for better credit-quality bonds, does not differ greatly from the conventional asset-swap spread. The Z-spread is usually the higher spread of the two, following the logic of spot rates, but not always. If it differs greatly, then the bond can be considered to be mispriced.

FIGURE 2.3 is the Bloomberg screen YAS for the same bond shown in Figure 2.2, as of the same date. It shows a number of spreads for the bond. The main spread of 151.00 basis points (bps) is the spread over the government yield curve. This is an interpo-lated spread, as can be seen lower down the screen, with the appro-priate benchmark bind identified. We see that the asset-swap spread is 121.6 bps, while the Z-spread is 118.8 bps. When undertaking relative value analysis, for instance if making comparisons against cash funding rates or the same company name CDS, it is this lower spread that should be used.[3]

---

3. On the date in question, the 10-year CDS for this reference entity was quoted as 96.8 bps, which is a rare example of a negative basis—in this case, −22 bps.

FIGURE 2.3 *Bloomberg page YAS for GKN bond, August 10, 2005*

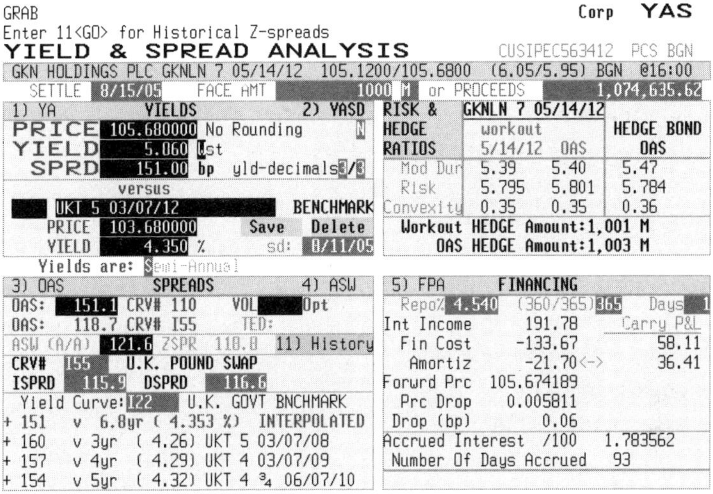

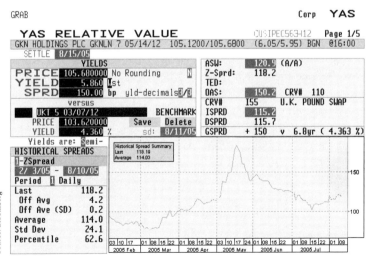

FIGURE 2.4 *Bloomberg page YAS for GKN bond, August 10, 2005,
showing Z-spread history*

Source: Bloomberg

The same screen can be used to check spread history. This is shown in **FIGURE 2.4**, the Z-spread graph for the GKN bond for the 6 months prior to our calculation date.

The Z-spread is closely related to the bond price, as shown by

$$P = \sum_{i=1}^{n} \left[\frac{C_i + M_i}{\left(1 + \left((Z + S_i + T_i)/m\right)\right)^i} \right], \qquad (2.2)$$

where

    n is the number of interest periods until maturity

    P is the bond price

    C is the coupon

    M is the redemption payment (so bond cash flow is all C plus M)

    Z is the Z-spread

    m is the frequency of coupon payments.

In effect, this is the standard bond price equation with the discount rate adjusted by whatever the Z-spread is; it is an iterative calculation. The appropriate maturity swap rate is used, which is the essential difference between the I-spread and the Z-spread. This is deemed to be more accurate, because the entire swap curve is taken into account rather than just one point on it. In practice, though, as we have seen in the example above, there is often little difference between the two spreads.

To reiterate, then, using the correct Z-spread, the sum of the bond's discounted cash flows will be equal to the current price of the bond.

We illustrate the Z-spread calculation in **FIGURE 2.5** (see pages 46 and 47). This is done using a hypothetical bond, the XYZ PLC 5% of June 2008, a 3-year bond at the time of the calculation. Market rates for swaps, Treasury, and CDS are also shown. We require the spread over the swaps curve that equates the present values of the cash flows to the current market price. The cash flows are discounted using the appropriate swap rate for each cash-flow maturity. With a bond yield of 5.635%, we see that the I-spread is 43.5 basis points, while the Z-spread is

19.4 basis points. In practice, the difference between these two spreads is rarely this large.

For readers' benefit, we also show the Excel formula in Figure 2.5. This shows how the Z-spread is calculated; for ease of illustration, we have assumed that the calculation takes place for value on a coupon date, so that we have precisely an even period to maturity.

The Asset-Swap CDS Price

Credit default swaps provide an efficient means of pricing pure credit, and by definition are a measure of the credit risk of a specific reference entity or reference asset. Asset swaps are well established in the market, and are used both to transform the cash-flow structure of a corporate bond and to hedge against interest-rate risk of a holding in such a bond. Because asset swaps are priced at a spread over Libor, with Libor representing interbank risk, the asset-swap spread represents in theory the credit risk of the asset-swap name. By the same token, using the no-arbitrage principle, it can be shown that the price of a credit default swap for a specific reference name should equate the asset-swap spread for the same name. However a number of factors, both structural and operational, combine to make credit default swaps trade at a different level to asset swaps. These factors are investigated in greater detail in Chapter 3. This difference in spread is the credit default swap basis, and can be either positive (the credit default swap trading above the asset-swap level) or negative (trading below the asset-swap level).

Asset-Swap Pricing

At the inception of the market, credit derivatives were valued using the asset-swap pricing technique. We will explain shortly why this approach is no longer used. Let us first consider, however, the theoretical reason why they *should* be priced using this approach.

A par asset swap typically combines the sale of an asset such

FIGURE 2.5 *Calculating the Z-spread, hypothetical 5% 2008 bond issued by XYZ PLC*

A1	B	C	D	E	F
2	**Issuer**	**XYZ PLC**			
3	Settlement date	6/1/05			
4	Maturity date	6/1/08			
5	Coupon	5%		**YIELD**	**0.05635**
6	Price	98.95		[Cell formula =YIELD(C4,C5,C6,C7,C8,C9,C1C	
7	Par	100			
8	Semiannual coupon	2		**PRICE**	**98.95000**
9	act/act	1		[Cell formula =PRICE(C4,C5,C6,C6,C8,C9,C1C	
10					
11	Bond yield	5.635%			
12	Sovereign bond yield	4.880%			
13	Swap rate	5.200%			
14					
15	3-year CDS price	28 bps			
16					
17	**Treasury spread**				
18	5.635–4.88	55 bps			
19					
20	**I-spread**				
21	5.635–5.20	43.5 bps			
22					
23	**Z-spread**	19.4 bps		0.00194	
24	The Z-spread (Z) is found using iteration.				
25					
26					
27	Cash-flow date	12/1/05		6/1/06	12/1/06
28	Cash-flow maturity (years)	0.50		1.00	1.50
29	0.5-year swap rate (S)	4.31%		4.84%	4.99%
30	Cash flow (CF)	2.50		2.50	2.50
31	Discount factor	0.97797598		0.951498751	0.926103469
32	(DF Calculation)	1/(1+(S+Z)/2)^1		1/(1+(S+Z)/2)^2	1/(1+(S+Z)/2)^3
33	CF present value (PV)	2.445		2.379	2.315
34					
35					
36					
37	A Z-spread of 19.4 basis points gives us the current bond price so is the correct one.				
38	Using this value, the sum of all the discounted cash flows is equal to the market pri•				
39					
40	**CDS Basis**				
41	28–19.4	8.6 bps			
42	The basis is positive in this example.				

G	H	I	
			Sum of PVs
6/1/07	12/1/07	6/1/08	
2.00	2.50	3.00	
5.09%	5.18%	5.20%	
2.50	2.50	102.50	
0.900947692	0.875835752	0.852419659	
1/(1+(S+Z)/2)^4	1/(1+(S+Z)/2)^5	1/(1+(S+Z)/2)^6	
2.252	2.190	87.373	**98.95**

as a fixed-rate corporate bond to a counterparty, at par and with no interest accrued, with an interest-rate swap. The coupon on the bond is paid in return for Libor, plus a spread if necessary. This spread is the asset-swap spread and is the price of the asset swap. In effect, the asset swap allows market participants that pay Libor-based funding to receive the asset-swap spread. This spread is a function of the credit risk of the underlying bond asset, which is why it could be viewed as equivalent to the price payable on a credit default swap written on that asset.

The generic pricing is given by

$$Y_a = Y_b - ir, \qquad (2.3)$$

where

Y_a is the asset-swap spread
Y_b is the asset spread over the benchmark
ir is the interest-rate swap spread.

The asset spread over the benchmark is simply the bond (asset) redemption yield over that of the government benchmark. The interest-rate swap spread reflects the cost involved in converting fixed-coupon benchmark bonds into a floating-rate coupon during the life of the asset (or default swap), and is based on the swap rate for that maturity.

The theoretical basis for deriving a default swap price from the asset-swap rate can be illustrated by looking at a basis-type trade involving a cash market reference asset (bond) and a default swap written on this bond. This is similar in concept to the risk-neutral, or *no-arbitrage*, concept used in derivatives pricing. The theoretical trade involves:

❑ A long position in the cash market floating-rate note (FRN) priced at par, and which pays a coupon of Libor + X basis points

❑ A long position (bought protection) in a default swap written on the same FRN, of identical term-to-maturity and at a cost of Y basis points

The buyer of the bond is able to fund the position at Libor. In other words, the bondholder has the following net cash flow:

$$(100 - 100) + \big((\text{Libor} + X) - (\text{Libor} + Y)\big)$$

or $X - Y$ basis points.

In the event of default, the bond is delivered to the protection seller in return for payment of par, enabling the bondholder to close out the funding position. During the term of the trade, the bondholder has earned $X - Y$ basis points while assuming no credit risk. For the trade to meet the no-arbitrage condition, we must have $X = Y$. If $X \neq Y$, the investor would be able to establish the position and generate a risk-free profit.

This is a logically tenable argument as well as a reasonable assumption. The default risk of the cash bondholder is identical in theory to that of the default seller. In the next section, we illustrate an asset-swap pricing example, before looking at why in practice there exist differences in pricing between default swaps and cash market reference assets.

Asset-Swap Pricing Example

XYZ PLC is a Baa2-rated corporate. The 7-year asset swap for this entity is currently trading at 93 basis points; the underlying 7-year bond is hedged by an interest-rate swap with an AA2-rated bank. The risk-free rate for floating-rate bonds is Libid minus 12.5 basis points (assume the bid-offer spread is 6 basis points). This suggests that the credit spread for XYZ PLC is 111.5 basis points. The credit spread is the return required by an investor for holding the credit of XYZ PLC. The protection seller is conceptually long the asset, and so would short the asset to hedge its position. This is illustrated in **FIGURE 2.6**. The price charged for the default swap is the price of shorting the asset, which works out as 111.5 basis points each year.

Therefore, we can price a credit default written on XYZ PLC as the present value of 111.5 basis points for 7 years, discounted

FIGURE 2.6 *Credit default swap and asset-swap hedge*

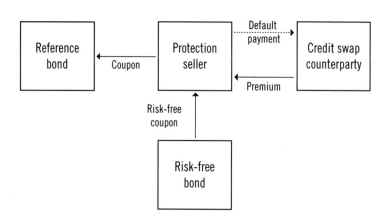

at the interest-rate swap rate of 5.875%. This computes to a
credit swap price of 6.25%.

Reference	XYZ PLC
Term	7 years
Interest-rate swap rate	5.875%
Asset swap	Libor plus 93 bps
Default swap pricing:	
Benchmark rate	Libid minus 12.5 bps
Margin	6 bps
Credit default swap	111.5 bps
Default swap price	6.252%

Pricing Differentials

A number of factors observed in the market serve to make the price
of credit risk that has been established synthetically using default
swaps to differ from its price as traded in the cash market. In fact,
identifying (or predicting) such differences gives rise to arbitrage
opportunities that may be exploited by basis trading in the cash

and derivative markets.[4] These factors include the following:

❑ Bond identity: the bondholder is aware of the exact issue that he is holding in the event of default; however, default swap sellers may receive potentially any bond from a basket of deliverable instruments that rank pari passu with the cash asset; this is the delivery option afforded the long swap holder.

❑ The borrowing rate for a cash bond in the repo market may differ from Libor if the bond is to any extent *special*; this does not impact the default swap price, which is fixed at inception.

❑ Certain bonds rated AAA (such as U.S. agency securities) sometimes trade below Libor in the asset-swap market; however, a bank writing protection on such a bond will expect a premium (positive spread over Libor) for selling protection on the bond.

❑ Depending on the precise reference credit, the default swap may be more liquid than the cash bond, resulting in a lower default swap price, or less liquid than the bond, resulting in a higher price.

❑ Credit default swaps may be required to pay out on credit events that are technical defaults, and not the full default that impacts a cash bondholder; protection sellers may demand a premium for this additional risk.

❑ The credit default swap buyer is exposed to counterparty risk during the term of the trade, unlike the cash bondholder.

For these and other reasons, the default swap price often differs from the cash market price for the same asset. Therefore, banks are increasingly turning to credit pricing models, based on the same models used to price interest-rate derivatives, when pricing credit derivatives.

Illustration Using the BLOOMBERG PROFESSIONAL® Service

Observations from the market show the difference in price between asset swaps on a bond and a credit default swap written on

---

4. The reasons for this differential, and the way basis trades are conducted, are shown in Chapters 3 and 6.

FIGURE 2.7 *Bloomberg page DES for Air Products & Chemicals bond*

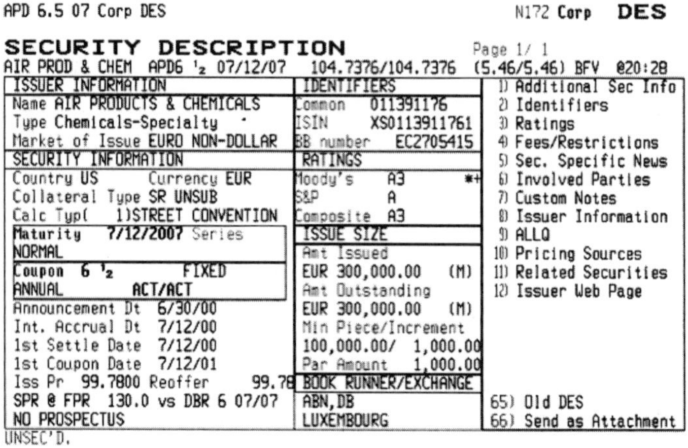

```
APD 6.5 07 Corp DES                                    N172 Corp  DES
SECURITY DESCRIPTION                          Page 1/ 1
AIR PROD & CHEM   APD6 ½ 07/12/07    104.7376/104.7376   (5.46/5.46) BFV  @20:28
┌─ISSUER INFORMATION────────┬─IDENTIFIERS──────────────┐ 1) Additional Sec Info
│Name AIR PRODUCTS & CHEMICALS│Common    011391176      │ 2) Identifiers
│Type Chemicals-Specialty   ·│ISIN      XS0113911761    │ 3) Ratings
│Market of Issue EURO NON-DOLLAR│BB number   EC2705415  │ 4) Fees/Restrictions
├─SECURITY INFORMATION──────┼─RATINGS──────────────────┤ 5) Sec. Specific News
│Country US     Currency EUR│Moody's       A3       **│ 6) Involved Parties
│Collateral Type SR UNSUB   │S&P           A          │ 7) Custom Notes
│Calc Typ( 1)STREET CONVENTION│Composite   A3          │ 8) Issuer Information
│Maturity      7/12/2007 Series├─ISSUE SIZE─────────────┤ 9) ALLQ
│NORMAL                     │Amt Issued               │ 10) Pricing Sources
│Coupon  6 ½         FIXED  │EUR 300,000.00     (M)   │ 11) Related Securities
│ANNUAL          ACT/ACT    │Amt Outstanding          │ 12) Issuer Web Page
│Announcement Dt  6/30/00   │EUR 300,000.00     (M)   │
│Int. Accrual Dt  7/12/00   │Min Piece/Increment      │
│1st Settle Date  7/12/00   │100,000.00/  1,000.00    │
│1st Coupon Date  7/12/01   │Par Amount   1,000.00    │
│Iss Pr  99.7800 Reoffer   99.78├─BOOK RUNNER/EXCHANGE──┤
│SPR @ FPR  130.0 vs DBR 6 07/07│ABN,DB               │ 65) Old DES
│NO PROSPECTUS              │LUXEMBOURG               │ 66) Send as Attachment
│UNSEC'D.                   │                         │
└───────────────────────────┴─────────────────────────┘
```

Source: Bloomberg

that bond, reflecting the factors stated in the previous section. We illustrate this now using a euro-denominated corporate bond.

The bond is the Air Products & Chemicals 6½% bond due July 2007. This bond is rated A3/A as shown in **FIGURE 2.7**, the description page from the Bloomberg. The asset-swap price for that specific bond to its term to maturity as of January 18, 2002, was 41.6 basis points. This is shown in **FIGURE 2.8**. The relevant swap curve used as the pricing reference is indicated on the screen as curve 45, which is the Bloomberg reference number for the euro swap curve and is shown in **FIGURE 2.9**.

We now consider the credit default swap page on the Bloomberg for the same bond, which is shown in **FIGURE 2.10**. For the similar maturity range, the credit default swap price would be approximately 115 basis points. This differs significantly from the asset-swap price.

From the screen, we can see that the benchmark curve is the same as that used in the calculation shown in Figure 2.9. The corporate curve used as the pricing reference, however, is indicated as the euro-denominated U.S.-issuer A3 curve, and this is

FIGURE 2.8 *Asset-swap calculator on Bloomberg page ASW, January 18, 2002*

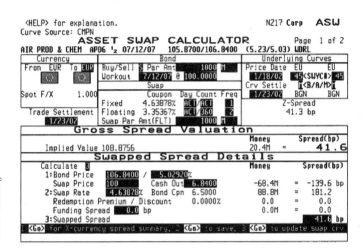

FIGURE 2.9 *Euro swap curve on Bloomberg page SWDF as of January 18, 2002*

<HELP> for explanation, <MENU> for similar functions.   N217 Corp   SWDF
Screen Printed

New Euro Currency   SWAP CURVE

	Cash Rates			Type 0 <page> to view more cash rates.				
Term	1 wk	1 mo	2 mo	3 mo	4 mo	5 mo	6 mo	9 mo	1 yr
Bid	3.3420	3.3490	3.3460	3.3450	3.3470	3.3490	3.3510	3.3890	3.5060
Ask	3.3420	3.3490	3.3460	3.3450	3.3470	3.3490	3.3510	3.3890	3.5360
Updt	10:02	10:02	10:02	10:02	10:02	10:02	10:02	10:02	18:00

				Swap Rates					
Term	18 mo	2 yr	30 mo	3 yr	4 yr	5 yr	6 yr	7 yr	8 yr
Bid	3.6910	3.8970		4.1800	4.3780	4.5500	4.7000	4.8300	4.9280
Ask	3.7060	3.9270		4.2100	4.3980	4.5700	4.7300	4.8500	4.9480
Updt	17:31	18:00		18:00	17:59	17:59	18:00	18:02	18:02
Src	CMPN	CMPN		CMPN	CMPN	CMPN	CMPN	CMPN	CMPN

			Long Term Swap Rates					
Term	9 yr	10 yr	11 yr	12 yr	15 yr	20 yr	25 yr	30 yr
Bid	5.0050	5.0650		5.1700	5.2780	5.3550	5.3600	5.3530
Ask	5.0250	5.0850		5.1900	5.2980	5.3750	5.3900	5.3730
Updt	18:02	18:02		18:02	18:02	18:02	18:00	18:02
Src	CMPN	CMPN		CMPN	CMPN	CMPN	CMPN	CMPN

Daytype / Frequency Conventions   IRSB <Go> for Sprd vrs Benchmark
Cash Rates   ACT/360
Swap Rates   30/360 , 1   Enter <Menu> to select another crv
                                             For old SWYC, enter SWYC OLD <GO>.

FIGURE 2.10 *Default swap page CDSW for Air Products &*
Chemicals bond, January 18, 2002

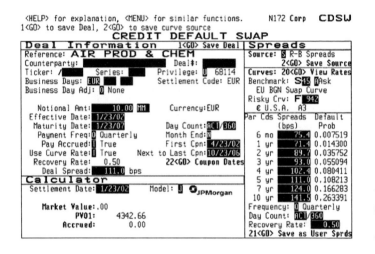

FIGURE 2.11 *Fair market curve, euro A3 sector*

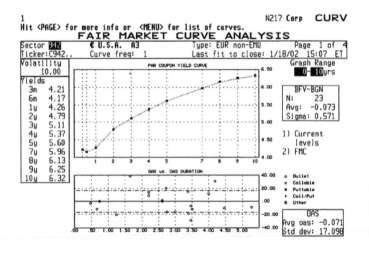

FIGURE 2.12 *Fair market curve, euro Banks A3 sector*

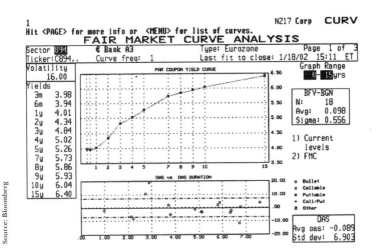

Source: Bloomberg

shown in **FIGURE 2.11**. This is page CURV on the Bloomberg, and is the fair value corporate credit curve constructed from a basket of A3 credits. On the following pages of the same screen, the user can view the list of bonds that are used to construct the curve. For comparison, we also show the Bank A3-rated corporate credit yield curve in **FIGURE 2.12**.

Prices observed in the market will invariably show this pattern of difference between the asset-swap price and the credit default swap price. The page CDSW on the Bloomberg uses the generic risky curve to calculate the default swap price, and adds the credit spread to the interest-rate swap curve. However, the ASW page is the specific asset-swap rate for that particular bond, to the bond's term to maturity; this is another reason why the prices of the two instruments will differ significantly.

On the Bloomberg, the user can select either the JPMorgan credit default swap pricing model or a generic discounted credit spreads model. These are indicated by "J" or "D" in the box marked "Model" on the CDSW page. **FIGURE 2.13** shows this

FIGURE 2.13 *CDSW page with discounted spreads model selected*

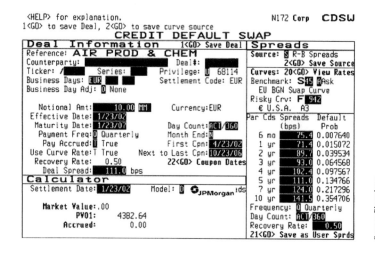

Source: Bloomberg

page with the generic model selected. Although there is no difference in the swap prices, the default probabilities, as expected, have changed under this setting.

Our example illustrates the difference in swap price that we discussed earlier, and can be observed for any number of corporate credits across sectors. This suggests that middle-office staff and risk managers that use the asset-swap technique to independently value default swap books are at risk of obtaining values that differ from those in the market. This is an important issue for credit derivative market-making banks.

Cash-CDS Basis

We see then that the basis is the CDS spread minus the ASW spread. Alternatively, it can be the CDS spread minus the Z-spread. So the basis is given by

$$B = D - CashSpread, \qquad (2.4)$$

FIGURE **2.14** *Bloomberg graph using screen G <Go>, plot of asset-swap spread and CDS price for GKN bond, April–September 2005*

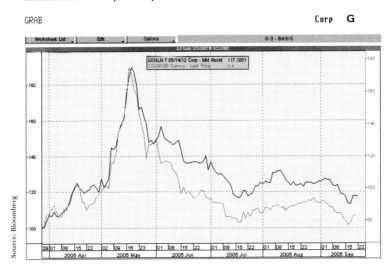

Source: Bloomberg

where D is the CDS price. Where $D - CashSpread > 0$, it is a positive basis; the opposite is a negative basis.

FIGURE 2.14 shows page G <Go> on the Bloomberg, set up to show the Z-spread and CDS price history for the GKN 2012 bond for the period March–September 2005. We can select the "Table" option to obtain the actual values, which can then be used to plot the basis. This is shown in **FIGURE 2.15**, for the period August 22 to September 22, 2005. Notice how the basis was always negative during August–September; we see from Figure 2.14 that earlier in the year, the basis had briefly been positive. Changes in the basis give rise to arbitrage opportunities between the cash and synthetic markets. This is discussed in greater detail in Choudhry (2004b).

A wide range of factors drive the basis; these factors are described in detail in Chapter 3. The existence of a non–zero basis has implications for investment strategy. For instance, when the basis

FIGURE 2.15 *GKN bond, CDS basis during August–*
September 2005

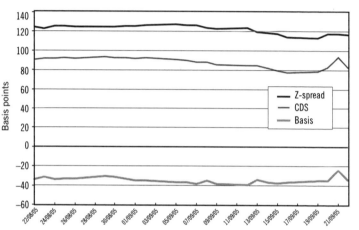

is negative, investors may prefer to hold the cash bond; whereas, if—for liquidity, supply, or other reasons—the basis is positive, the investor may wish to hold the asset synthetically, by selling protection using a credit default swap. Another approach is to arbitrage between the cash and synthetic markets, in the case of a negative basis by buying the cash bond and shorting it synthetically by buying protection in the CDS market. Investors have a range of spreads to use when performing their relative value analysis.

References

Choudhry, M., D. Joannas, R. Pienaar, and R. Pereira. 2001. *Capital market instruments: Analysis and valuation.* Upper Saddle River, NJ: FT Prentice Hall.

Choudhry, M. 2004a. *Structured credit products: Credit derivatives and synthetic securitisation.* Singapore: John Wiley & Sons.

———. 2004b. The credit default swap basis: Analysing the relationship between cash and synthetic markets. *Journal of Derivatives Use, Trading and Regulation* 10 (1) (June): 9–26.

CHAPTER 3

The CDS Basis I:
The Relationship Between Cash and Synthetic Credit Markets

Anyone composing a history of banking would observe that the use of interest-rate derivatives increased liquidity in the world's financial markets. Such instruments made it easier for users and providers of capital to price and hedge cash market debt capital products. Interest-rate swaps are now a leading indicator of the financial markets and a tool by which cash market efficiency is maintained. We can observe a similar happening in credit markets. Credit derivatives were introduced around 1994–1995, although liquid markets did not develop until a few years after that. They are now an important part of the global capital markets, and have contributed to increased liquidity in the cash credit market. They also enable market participants to price credit as an explicit asset class.

The growth of the credit derivatives market has produced a highly liquid market in credit default swaps across the credit curve. This liquidity in turn has helped to generate further growth in the market. There is a wide range of users of credit default swaps, from banks and other financial institutions to corporate and supranational bodies. The liquid nature of the credit default swap market has resulted in many investors accessing synthetic, rather than cash, markets in corporate credit. As well as greater liquidity, the synthetic market also offers investors the opportunity to access any part of the credit term structure, and not just those parts of the term structure where corporate borrowers have issued bonds. The liquidity of the synthetic market has resulted in many investors accessing both the credit derivatives and the cash bond markets to meet their investment requirements.

Because the synthetic market in credit is a reliable indicator of the cash market in credit, it is important for all market participants to be familiar with the two-way relationship between the two markets. The relationship is represented by the credit default swap *basis*: a measure of the difference in price and value between the cash and synthetic credit markets. This chapter is a review of the basis, and an assessment of the relationship between the two markets.

This chapter considers the close relationship between the synthetic and cash markets in credit. This relationship manifests itself most clearly in the shape of the credit default swap *basis*. We look at why the synthetic market price will differ necessarily from the cash market price. We then consider the factors that drive the basis, before looking at the implications this has for market participants.

The Market Differential

For a large number of corporate—and certain sovereign—names, the liquidity of the credit derivative market frequently exceeds that available for the same reference names in the cash market.[1] It is this feature that has enabled fund managers to exploit their expertise in credit trading by originating synthetic collateralized debt obligation (CDO) vehicles that enable them to arbitrage between cash and synthetic markets; for instance, see Fabozzi and Goodman (2001) and Choudhry (2002). As well as greater liquidity, the synthetic market also offers investors the oppor-

---

1. For instance, see RISK, Robeco CSO, May 2002. The asset-swap market is described as being part of the cash market, despite the fact that an interest-rate derivative (the swap element) is part of an asset swap.

tunity to access any part of the credit term structure, and not just those parts of the term structure where corporate borrowers have issued paper. The liquidity of the synthetic market has resulted in many investors accessing both the credit derivatives and the cash bond markets to meet their investment requirements.

In the previous chapter, we described the asset-swap approach to valuing credit default swap (CDS) contracts, which was used at the start of the market. We illustrated the no-arbitrage argument that indicated why this should be the case. In practice, the CDS spread will differ from the asset-swap (ASW) spread, and this has important implications for market participants in both cash and synthetic credit markets. Middle-office desks and risk managers that use the asset-swap technique to independently value default swap books are at risk of obtaining values that differ from those in the market. This is an important issue for credit derivative market-making banks.

There are a number of reasons why the cash market spread differs from the same reference asset credit default swap premium. This is noted, for instance, in Choudhry (2001) and Bomfim (2002). The latter illustrates the divergence of ASW and CDS spreads using financial entity and industrial entity reference names. The divergence is greatest with the industrial names considered in Bomfim's article.

The Credit Default Swap Basis

Although the theoretical case can be made as to why the CDS price should be equal to the ASW price, market observation tells us that this is not the case. This difference in pricing between the cash and synthetic markets was noted in the previous section, and results from the impact of a combination of factors. In essence, it is because credit derivatives isolate and trade credit as their sole asset, separately from any funding consideration, that they are priced at a different level than the asset swap on the same reference asset. There are other important factors, however, that must be considered, which we consider shortly.

FIGURE 3.1 *Selected reference name credit default swap and asset-swap spreads, May 2003*

REFERENCE CREDIT	CREDIT RATING	CDS SPREAD	ASSET-SWAP SPREAD (LIBOR-PLUS)	BASIS
Financials				
Ford Motor Credit	A2/A	59.3	51.1	+8.2
Household Finance	A2/A	72.2	57.2	+15.0
JPMorgan Chase	Aa3/AA–	89.0	66.9	+22.1
Merrill Lynch	Aa3/AA–	108.1	60.4	+47.7
Industrials				
AT&T Corp.	Baa2/BBB+	224.0	217.6	+6.4
FedEx Corp.	Baa2/BBB+	499.0	481.2	+17.8
General Motors	A3/BBB	205.1	237.7	**-32.6**
IBM (6-year callable bond)	A1/A+	27.2	8.2	+19.0
IBM (4-year callable bond)	A1/A+	33.3	11.0	+22.3

Bonds used are 5-year conventional bullet bonds.
CDS is 5-year maturity.
AT&T is 4-year maturity.
FedEx is 3-year maturity.

Rates source: Bloomberg

The difference between the CDS and the ASW price is known as the basis. The basis is given by

$$\text{credit default spread } (D) - \text{the asset-swap spread } (S). \quad (3.1)$$

Where $D - S > 0$, we have a *positive basis*. A positive basis occurs when the credit derivative trades higher than the asset-swap price, and is common. Where $D - S < 0$, we have a *negative basis*. This describes where the credit derivative trades tighter than the cash bond asset-swap spread.[2]

FIGURE 3.1 shows the basis for a sample of reference credits during May 2003. We use mid-prices for 5-year CDS and ASW for each name. The sample reflects the customary market state, with a positive basis for all but one of the names.

We illustrate further the different trading levels by looking at two issuer names in the Euromarkets, Telefonica and Fiat. **FIGURE 3.2** shows the yield spread levels for a selection of U.S. dollar bonds and Eurobonds issued by Telefonica, as of November 2002. We note that the credit default swap price is at levels comparable with the cheapest bond in the group, the 7.35% 2005 bond, issued in U.S. dollars.

A similar picture emerges when looking at a group of Fiat bonds, also from November 2002, as shown in **FIGURE 3.3**. Note that the credit curve given by the credit default swap prices inverts. This is because a year earlier, Fiat had issued a very large size "exchangeable" bond that had a July 2004 put date. The basis, previously flat, widened to over 100 basis points due to market makers hedging this bond with convertible bonds of the same name.

The basis will fluctuate in line with market sentiment on the particular credit. For instance, for a worsening credit, the basis

---

2. At this stage, we state the formal definition of the credit default swap bond basis as being the difference between the credit default spread and the par bond floating-rate spread of the same reference asset, the latter as expressed for an asset swap on the bond.

FIGURE **3.2** *Telefonica bond asset-swap and credit default swap spread levels, November 2002*

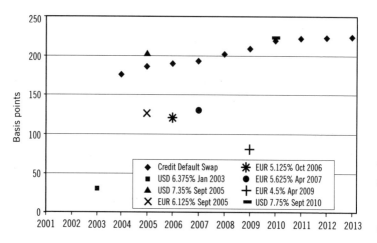

FIGURE **3.3** *Fiat bond asset-swap and credit default swap spread levels, November 2002*

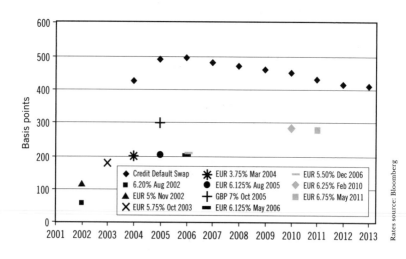

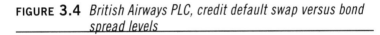

FIGURE 3.4 *British Airways PLC, credit default swap versus bond spread levels*

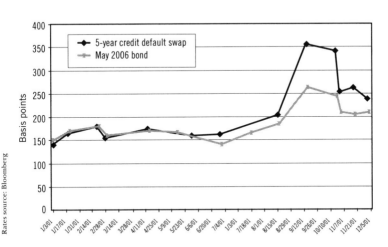

Rates source: Bloomberg

can become positive quite quickly. This is illustrated in **FIGURE 3.4**, which shows the widening in spread between the 5-year credit default swap levels with the similar-maturity May 2006 bond of the same name (in this case, British Airways PLC). The impact of the deteriorating business outlook in the last quarter of 2001 is prevalent, with the improving situation also illustrated toward the end of the year.

Factors Behind the Basis

The basis arises from a combination of factors, which we may group into:
- ❑ Technical factors
- ❑ Market factors

Technical factors, which are also referred to in the market variously as *fundamental* or *contractual* factors, are issues related to the definition or specification of the reference asset and of the CDS contract. *Market* factors, which are also referred to as *trading* factors, relate to issues connected with the state of the market in which contracts and reference assets are traded. Each factor exerts an influence on the basis, forcing it wider or tighter; the actual market basis at any one time will reflect the impact of all these factors together. We consider them in detail next.

Technical Factors

Technical factors that will influence the size and direction of the basis include the following:

CDS premiums are above zero: the price of a CDS represents the premium paid by the protection buyer to the protection seller—in effect an insurance premium. As such, it is always positive. Certain bonds rated AAA (such as U.S. agency securities, World Bank bonds, or German Pfandbriefe) frequently trade below Libor in the asset-swap market; this reflects the market view of credit risk associated with these names as being very low and also better than bank quality. A bank writing protection on such a bond, however, will expect a premium (positive spread over Libor) for selling protection on the bond. This will lead to a positive basis.

Greater protection level of the CDS contract: credit default swaps are frequently required to pay out on credit events that are technical defaults, and not the full default that impacts a cash bondholder. Protection sellers will therefore demand a premium for this additional risk, which makes the CDS trade above the ASW spread.

Bond identity and the delivery option: many CDS contracts that are physically settled name a reference *entity* rather than a specific reference asset. On occurrence of a credit event, the protection buyer often has a choice of deliverable assets with which to effect settlement. The looser the definition of deliverable asset is in the CDS contract documents, the larger the potential delivery basket: as long as the bond meets prespecified requirements for seniority and maturity, it may be delivered. Contrast this with the position of the bondholder in the cash market, who is aware of the exact issue that he is holding in the event of default. Default swap sellers, on the other hand, may receive potentially any bond from the basket of deliverable instruments that rank pari passu with the cash asset—this is the delivery option afforded the long swap holder. In practice therefore, the protection buyer will deliver the *cheapest-to-deliver* bond from the delivery basket, exactly as he would for an exchange-traded futures contract. This delivery option has debatable value in theory, but can have significant value in practice. For instance, the bonds of a specific obligor that might be trading cheaper in the market include:

❑ The bond with the lowest coupon
❑ A convertible bond
❑ An illiquid bond
❑ An asset-backed security (ABS) bond compared to a conventional fixed-coupon bond
❑ A very-long-dated bond

Following experience in the U.S. market (see Tolk [2001]), the United States adopted "modified restructuring" as one of the definitions of a credit event, which specifically restricts the delivery of long-dated bonds where restructuring is the credit event that triggers a contract payout. Nevertheless the last-named item is still relevant in the European market.

We see then that the delivery option therefore does carry value in the market. Similarly, for an option contract, this value increases the closer the contract holder gets to the "strike price," which for a CDS is a credit event. Market sentiment on the particular reference name will drive the basis more or less positive, depending on how favorably the name is viewed. As the credit quality of the reference name worsens, protection sellers will quote higher CDS premiums; the basis will also widen as the probability of a credit event increases. This is illustrated in **FIGURE 3.5**, the basis graph for AT&T. In March 2002, the firm was rated A2/A. By October, the CDS spread had widened considerably, and in common with other firms in its sector whose telecoms customers had reduced expenditure, its rating has been downgraded to Baa2/BBB+.

FIGURE 3.5 *AT&T basis: increasing as perceived credit quality worsens*

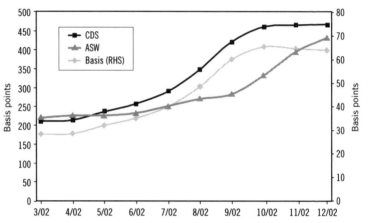

Rates source: Bloomberg

Where the opposite has occurred, and firms are upgraded as credit quality improves, the market has observed a narrowing basis.

As a consequence of all these factors, protection sellers will demand a higher premium for taking on a long position synthetically compared to a cash position.

Accrued coupon: this factor may be associated with cash- or physically settled contracts. In certain cases, the reference bond accrued coupon is also delivered to the protection buyer in the event of default. This has the effect of driving the CDS premium (and hence the basis) higher.

Assets trading above or below par: unlike a long cash bond position, a CDS contract provides protection on the entire par value of the reference asset. On occurrence of a credit event, the CDS payout will be par minus the recovery value (or minus the asset price at the time of default). If the asset is not trading at par, this payout will either over- or undercompensate the protection buyer, depending on whether the asset is trading at a premium or discount to par. So if the bond is trading at a discount, the protection seller will experience a greater loss than that suffered by an investor who is holding the cash bond. For instance, an investor who pays $90 per $100 nominal to buy a cash bond has less value at risk than an investor who has written CDS protection on the same bond. If the bond obligor defaults, and a recovery value for the bond is set at $30, the cash investor will have lost $60 while the CDS seller will have lost $70. As a result, the CDS price will trade at a higher level than the asset-swap price for the same asset where this is trading below par, leading to a larger basis.

The reverse applies for assets trading above par. If the reference asset is trading at a premium, the loss suffered by a CDS seller will be lower than that of the cash bondholder. This has the effect of driving the basis lower.

Funding versus Libor:[3] the funding cost of a bond plays a significant part in any trading strategy associated with it in the cash market. As such, it is a key driver of the ASW spread. A cash bond investor will need to fund the position, and we take the bond's repo rate as its funding rate.[4] The funding rate, or the bond's *cost-of-carry*, will determine if it is worthwhile for the investor to buy and hold the bond. A CDS contract, however, is an unfunded credit derivative that assumes a Libor funding cost. So an investor who has a funding cost of Libor plus 25 basis points will view the following two investments as theoretically identical:

- ❏ Buying a floating-rate note priced at par and paying Libor plus 125 bps
- ❏ Selling a CDS contract on the same FRN at a premium of 100 bps

---

3. It is a moot point whether this is a technical factor or a market factor. *Funding risk* exists in the cash market, and does not exist in the CDS market: the risk that, having bought a bond for cash, the funding rate at which the cost of funds is renewed rises above the bond's cost-of-carry. This risk, if it is to be compensated in the cash (ASW) market, would demand a higher ASW spread, and hence would drive the basis lower.

4. This being market practice, even if the investor is a fund manager who has bought the bond outright: as the bondholder, he can repo out the bond, for which he will pay the repo rate on the borrowed funds. So the funding rate is always the bond's repo rate for purposes of analysis.

Thus, the funding cost in the market will influence the basis. If it did not, the above two strategies would no longer be identical and arbitrage opportunities would result. Hence a Libor-plus funding cost will drive the basis lower. Equally, the reverse applies if the funding cost of an asset is below Libor (or if the investor can fund the asset at sub-Libor), which factor was discussed earlier.

Another factor to consider is the extent of any "specialness" in the repo market.[5] The borrowing rate for a cash bond in the repo market will differ from Libor if the bond is to any extent *special*; this does not impact the default swap price, which is fixed at inception. This is more a market factor, however, which we consider in the next section.

Counterparty risk: the protection buyer in a CDS contract takes on the counterparty risk of the protection seller, which does not occur in the cash market. This exposure lasts for the life of the contract, and will be significant if, on occurrence of a credit event, the protection seller is unable to fulfill his commitments. This feature has the effect of driving down the basis, because to offset against this risk, the buyer will look to a CDS premium that is *below* the cash asset-swap spread. In addition, the protection buyer will wish to look for protection seller counterparties that have a low default correlation to the reference assets being protected, to further reduce counterparty risk exposure. For instance, the counterparty risk exposure of a protection buyer in a CDS contract is increased when the contract has been written by an investment bank on a bank that is also a CDS market maker.

On the other side, the protection seller is exposed to counterparty risk of the protection buyer. Should the latter default, the CDS contract will terminate. The protection seller will suffer a mark-to-market loss if the CDS premium has widened since trade inception.

---

5. If the repo rate for a specific bond is greater than around 20 bps lower than the "general collateral" rate for that asset class's repo rate, it is deemed special. The cost of funds payable by the holder of a special bond that is repo'ed out will be lower than Libor.

Legal risk associated with CDS contract documentation: this risk has been highlighted in a number of high-profile cases, where an unintendedly broad definition of "credit event," as stated in the contract documents, has exposed the protection seller to unexpected risks. Typically, this will be where a "credit event" has been deemed to occur beyond what might be termed a default or technical default. This occurred, for instance, with Conseco in the United States, as first discussed in Tolk (2001).

Associated with legal risk is documentation risk, the general risk that credit events and other terms of trade, as defined in the CDS documentation, may be open to dispute or arguments over interpretation. We can expect documentation risk to decrease as legal documentation is standardized across a larger number of shares. The 2003 International Swaps and Derivatives Association (ISDA) definitions also seek to address this issue.

Market Factors

Market factors that will influence the size and direction of the basis include the following:

Market demand: strong demand from protection buyers such as commercial banks protecting loan books, or insurance companies undertaking synthetic short selling trades, will drive the basis wider. Equally, strong market demand from protection sellers will drive the basis tighter.

Liquidity premium: the CDS for a particular reference asset may reflect a liquidity premium for that name. An investor seeking to gain exposure to that name can buy the bond in the cash market or sell protection on it in the CDS market. For illiquid maturities or terms, the protection seller may charge a premium. At the 2- to 5-year maturities, the CDS market is very liquid (as is the cash market). For some corporate names, however, cash market liquidity dries up toward the 10-year area. In addition, depending on the precise reference credit, the default swap may be more liquid than the cash bond, resulting in a lower default swap price, or less liquid than the bond, resulting in a higher price.

Liquidity in the cash market can be quite restricted for below-investment-grade names, and secondary market trading is usually confined to "current" issues. Similarly, to the repo market, the relationship flows both ways, and liquid names in the cash market are usually liquid names in the CDS market. For corporate names for whom no bonds exist, however, CDS contracts are the only way for investors to gain an exposure (see below).

Relative liquidity is also related to the next item on our list.

Shortage of cash assets: in some markets, it is easier to source a particular reference name or reference asset in the CDS market than in the cash market. This has always been the case in the loan market; although there has been a secondary market in loans in the United States for some time, it is relatively illiquid in Europe. In the bond market, it can be difficult to short some corporate bonds due to problems in covering the position in repo, and also the risk that the bonds go special in repo. When cash assets are difficult to short, traders and speculators can buy protection in the CDS market. This does not involve any short covering or repo risk, and also fixes the cost of "funding" (the CDS premium) at trade inception. The demand for undertaking this in CDS will have a positive impact on the basis.

The structured finance market: the rapid growth of the market in synthetic CDOs has both arisen out of, and driven, the liquidity of the CDS market. These products are considered in detail in Choudhry (2002) and Anson et al. (2004). Synthetic CDOs use CDS contracts to source reference credits in the market, and frequently make use of basket CDSs and a portfolio of credits. As investment vehicles, they sell protection on reference names. The counterparty to the CDO vehicle will hedge out its exposure in the CDS market. Large demand in the CDS market, arising from hedging requirements of CDO counterparties, impacts the basis and frequently drives it lower.

New market issuance: the impact of new bond and loan issues on the CDS basis illustrates the rapid acceptance of this instrument in the market, and its high level of liquidity. Where previously market participants would hedge new issues using interest-rate derivatives and/or government bonds, they now use CDSs as a more exact hedge against credit risk. The impact on the basis flows both ways, however, and may increase or decrease it, depending on specific factors. For example, new issues of corporate bonds enlarge the delivery basket for physically settled CDS contracts. This should widen the basis, but the cash market may also widen as well, as investors move into the new bonds. For loans, a new issue by banks is often hedged in the CDS market, and this should cause the basis to widen. Convertible bond issuance also tends to widen the basis; we noted earlier the impact of the issue of an exchangeable bond by Fiat on the CDS basis for that name.

The Basis Smile

If plotted graphically, the CDS-cash basis tends to exhibit a smile. This is illustrated in **FIGURE 3.6** and is known as the *basis smile*. This reflects a number of the features we have discussed above. The main reasons for the smile effect is that highly rated reference names, such as AA or higher, fund in the asset-swap market at sub-Libor. If an entity is buying protection on such a name, however, it will pay above-Libor premiums. The basis therefore

FIGURE 3.6 *Basis smile for industrial names, November 2002*

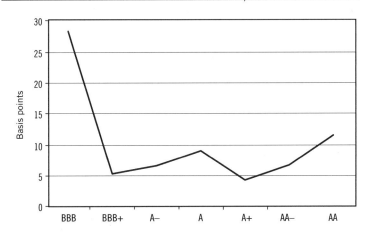

Source: JPMorgan Chase Bank

tends to increase with better quality names, and results in the smile effect. Other factors that impact the smile are the cheapest-to-deliver options for lower-rated credits.

The Dynamics of the Default Swap Basis

We consider now the interaction of the different factors that drive the basis.

Positive and Negative Basis Situations

At any time, the CDS basis will reflect the combined impact of all the above factors. Some of these will affect the basis with positive bias, whereas others will have a negative bias. Generally, technical and market factors that tend to drive the basis wider include:

- ❑ CDS premiums above zero
- ❑ The delivery option
- ❑ Accrued coupon
- ❑ Bond price below par
- ❑ Funding below Libor
- ❑ Legal and documentation risk
- ❑ Market liquidity
- ❑ New bond issuance
- ❑ Difficulty of shorting cash bonds

The factors that tend to drive the basis lower include:

- ❑ Counterparty risk
- ❑ Bonds priced above par
- ❑ Funding above Libor
- ❑ Impact of the structured finance market

A reversal of market circumstances, however, can lead to the same factor having a reverse impact. For instance, if a credit is viewed in the market as being of decreasing quality, factors such as the delivery option, bonds trading below par, difficulty in shorting the cash bond, and worsening liquidity will all push the basis wider. If the credit is viewed as improving in terms of quality, however, the impact of these factors will diminish (for instance, the delivery option has decreasing value as the probability of a credit event's occurring decreases).

The market norm is a positive basis, for all the reasons that we have discussed. Although some of the factors above do influence the basis toward a negative value, observation tells us that the market norm is a positive basis. The combination of all the various factors tends to result in a negative basis for reference names that are highly rated in terms of credit quality. This is because those factors that drive the basis lower carry greater influence for highly rated names. Specifically,

❏ the cash bond price is generally closer to par for high-quality credits; and

❏ the value of the delivery option is less, as there is less chance of default or credit event for AAA- and AA-rated names.

In addition, compared to sub-investment-grade names, highly rated names are more often selected as reference credits in synthetic CDOs. All these factors combine to drive the basis lower for good-quality names, and this sometimes leads to negative values.

As well as being relatively uncommon, a negative basis is usually temporary. It usually reflects a particular set of circumstances, which disappear over time. A negative basis also represents an arbitrage opportunity for market participants who can trade across cash and synthetic markets, which would return the basis to positive territory as soon as it was exploited in the market. We illustrate the temporary nature of the negative basis in **FIGURE 3.7**. This shows how the basis had reverted to positive for those sectors that had exhibited negative basis, within three months.

Market Observation of the Basis Trend

To illustrate the interplay between cash and synthetic markets, and the influence of all the above factors acting in concert, we show in **FIGURE 3.8** the ASW and CDS spreads for a sample of 100 investment-grade U.S. dollar–denominated corporate bonds,

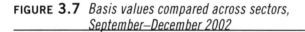

FIGURE 3.7 *Basis values compared across sectors, September–December 2002*

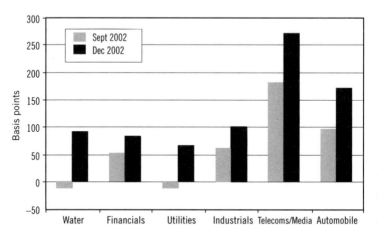

Source: Bloomberg

during June 2002 to January 2003. This shows the default swap basis trend during this period—with the overall basis staying positive on the whole, but moving between positive and negative.

We conclude from this observation that

❑ the overall default swap basis was essentially positive;

❑ the CDS spread volatility at least matches that of the cash market, and sometimes exceeds it;

❑ at times the basis moved with the cash spread, but not to the same extent, thus widening as the cash spread widened;

❑ there is a high degree of correlation between the two markets, as we would expect; and

❑ the basis itself moves in the direction of the market—in other words, we observe that the basis widens as cash and synthetic spreads widen.

We may conclude further, then, that the basis acts much as the repo rate acts in the cash bond market. The relationship between special rates in repo and bond prices moves both ways, and one can lead the other depending on circumstances (see Bank

Data sources: Bloomberg, CSFB, JPMorgan Chase Bank

FIGURE 3.8 *The dynamics of the credit default swap basis, 2002–2003*

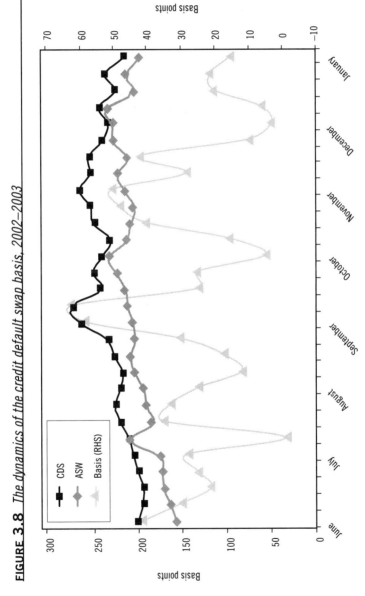

of England [1997]). The CDS market has a two-way relation-ship with the cash asset-swap market, and each will lead the other according to circumstance.

The iTraxx Index Basis[6]

The iTraxx and CDX indexes have developed into a reasonably liquid set of CDS contracts and as such are viewed as a key credit market indicator by investors. As a market benchmark, they can be taken to represent the market as a whole, similar to an equity index, and as such can provide a guide to the health of the credit market as well as imply market perception of future direction. Because there is an intrinsic "fair value" implied for the index, which differs from the actual market level at any time, there is also a CDS index basis that can be observed. Assessing this basis there-fore is an important part of an investor's relative value analysis of the market.

A CDS index basis arises because of the different approaches avail-able to valuing the index spread.[7] We can describe the following:

❑ *Theoretical spread:* This is the average of the single-name CDS spreads for all the constituent names in the index, weighted by probability of default.[8] It is also known as the *fair spread*.

❑ *Market spread:* This is the spread quoted for trading in the market. It is based on the theoretical spread, but adjusted us-ing a flat credit curve. It is also known as the *intrinsic spread* or the *real spread*.

There is also the *average spread*, which is simply the average

---

6. The author would like to thank Suraj Gohil for his invaluable assistance with this section. Any errors remain the sole responsibility of the author.

7. One is reminded again that a more accurate term for *spread* with respect to credit derivative prices is *premium*, particularly with respect to CDS prices, as the spread is not a spread over anything. However, the term is in common usage in the market.

8. Probability of Default (PD) = Spread$/(1 - R)$ where R is the recovery rate.

of all the constituent name CDS spreads equally weighted.

The index basis is given by

$$basis = market\ spread - theoretical\ spread.$$

From a relative value analysis point of view, we require a tractable means of calculating the two spreads or at least of measuring the basis. This is considered next.

The Index Spread

The theoretical spread is sometimes defined as the average spread, but this is not correct because it does not weight the constituent names' probability of default. In fact, the theoretical spread will differ from the average spread because of the nature of the construction of the index: An investor will receive the same spread for all reference names, whereas the average CDS spread of the constituent names will be different from this fixed spread.

Instead, we define the theoretical spread for a CDS written on the index as the spread that equates the net present value of the swap to zero. The expression for the spread is derived from the expression for the net present value of the CDS. The latter assumes—exactly as for an interest-rate swap—that the premium leg of the CDS is equal to the default leg. This is written as

$$Index_{NPV} = S_{Index}\frac{1}{N}\sum_{i=1}^{N}CS01_i - \frac{1}{N}\sum_{i=1}^{N}S_iCS01_i \quad (3.2)$$

where

S_{Index} is the index theoretical spread

S_i is the spread of CDS_i

$CS01_i$ is the credit risk exposure of CDS_i.

Note that $CS01$ is also referred to as risky-DV01, risky-PV01, or risky-PVBP. It is defined as the change in market value of a CDS contract for a 1-basis-point change in the CDS

EXAMPLE 3.1 *CDS mark-to-market risk exposure*

In Chapter 1, we described the approach to pricing a CDS contract. In essence, the CDS spread premium is that value that equates the net present value of the contract to zero, given our assumption that under no-arbitrage principles the fixed (premium) leg of the swap must equal the floating (default) leg. Therefore, we may write

$$(1-R)\sum_{k=1}^{K} DF_k PD_k = S\frac{1}{M}\sum_{k=1}^{K} DF_k(1-PD_k) \qquad (3.3)$$

where
- R is the recovery rate
- DF_k is the discount factor at time k
- PD_k is the probability of default at time k
- S is the CDS fixed spread (premium)
- M is the CDS premium payment frequency.

Note that $(1-PD_k)$ is the probability of survival to time k, which is given by the expression shown, although in certain texts it is written out as a separate expression.[9]

From (3.3) we can derive an expression for the CDS $CS01$, which is the main CDS risk exposure measure. $CS01$ is the change in market value of a CDS for a 1-basis-point change in the CDS spread, and is usually given by

$$CS01 = \frac{1}{M}\sum_{k=1}^{K} DF_k PS_k.$$

Some market practitioners refer to "risky-DV01" as the change in CDS value for a 1-basis-point parallel shift in the CDS credit-risky curve.

---

9. We would write $(1-PD_k) = PS_k$ where PS_k is the survival probability to time k. It is given by

$$PS_k = e^{-\sum_{k=1}^{K}\lambda_k(t_k-t_{k-1})}$$

where
  PS_k is the survival probability at time t_k
  λ_k is the default intensity between time t_{k-1} and time t_k, obtained by backing out default probabilities from the market-observed CDS curve.

premium.[10] The expression for the $CS01$ is given in the shaded box (see **EXAMPLE 3.1**).

Given (3.2), the expression for the index theoretical spread can be written as

$$S_{Index} = \frac{\sum_{i=1}^{N} S_i CS01_i}{\sum_{i=1}^{N} CS01_i}. \tag{3.4}$$

In general, the theoretical spread lies below the index pure average spread.

The market or real spread differs from the spread given by (3.4). The difference arises because market convention is to value the index CDS using a flat credit curve.[11] So we describe the market spread as that spread that makes the net present value for the contract, assuming a flat credit curve, equate to the net present value given by (3.4) above. So formally, for S_{Market} we write

$$\left(F - S_{Market}\right)CS01_{Flat} = \left(F - S_{Index}\right)\sum_{i=1}^{N} CS01_i \tag{3.5}$$

where

$$S_{Index} = \frac{\sum_{i=1}^{N} S_i CS01_i}{\sum_{i=1}^{N} CS01_i}$$

10. Strictly speaking, we define it as the change in contract market value for a 1-basis-point parallel shift in the credit curve. As with a bond instrument DV01, this is often taken as representing a change in market value for a 1-basis-point change in yield (bond) or CDS premium (CDS).

11. This is also the methodology employed by the CDSW screen on the Bloomberg.

F is the index fixed premium

$CS01_{Flat}$ is the $CS01$ calculated using a flat credit curve

$CS01_i$ is the $CS01$ of CDS_i calculated using the credit-risky curve for reference entity i.

In practice, the difference between the index theoretical spread and the market spread is not great, except for indexes composed of high-volatility names. From the expressions above, we can see that a key driver of the spread difference is the steepness of the credit-risky curves for each constituent name; the steeper the curve(s), the greater the difference between the two spreads. At any CDS spread level, a flatter credit-risky curve means a lower $CS01$.

The level of the index fixed premium also influences the difference: if the fixed premium lies above the theoretical spread, the market spread will be lower than the theoretical spread, and vice versa. This is because of the impact of the change in the market spread on the flat curve $CS01$, with increases in the spread reducing the $CS01$.

Market Observation

In practice, the basis in index CDS is small, with exceptions being observed for high-volatility indexes. We consider the June 2011 iTraxx investment-grade Europe index (series 5), which commenced trading in March 2006 as the 5-year benchmark. **FIGURE 3.9** shows the levels for the market and theoretical spreads for this index during March 2006–June 2006, while **FIGURE 3.10** shows the basis. Observe that the basis fluctuates from negative to positive and back, although the absolute values are small.

Irrespective of its absolute value, observing the basis enables investors to gauge perceived fair value for the index. By comparing the market spread against the theoretical spread, we can assess whether the index is trading at fair value or not. For instance, during June 2005 the iTraxx Europe crossover 5-year index was observed with a basis of around 13 basis points, which suggested mispricing of the index fair value. For comparison, we

FIGURE 3.9 *iTraxx IG Europe index CDS theoretical and market spreads, March–June 2006*

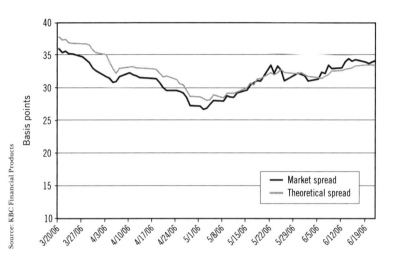

FIGURE 3.10 *iTraxx IG Europe index CDS basis*

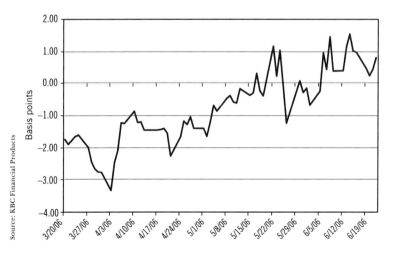

TABLE 3.1 *Index CDS basis for selected indexes, June 2006*

INDEX	BASIS POINTS				
	AVERAGE SPREAD	MARKET SPREAD	THEORETICAL SPREAD	AVERAGE SPREAD BASIS	THEORETICAL SPREAD BASIS
iTraxx IG Europe 5-year	44	43	44	−1	−1
iTraxx IG Europe High-Vol. 5-year	81	83	81	+2	+2
iTraxx Europe Crossover 5-year	349	350	337	+1	+13
CDX NA IG 5-year	63	59	61	−4	−2
CDX NA IG High-Vol. 5-year	139	133	133	−6	0

Source: Markit Partners

show the basis values for other indexes at the same time, with data reported by Markit Partners.

The Impact of the Basis on Trading Strategy

From the inception of trading in CDS, market participants have known that inefficiencies in pricing can result in arbitrage opportunities. Using CDS, the basic market neutral strategy (credit-risk free) is to buy the cash bond and swap it in the asset-swap market, and buy protection using CDS. The trader receives the bond coupon now as floating coupon, and pays the CDS premium. To match payment and receipt bases, the bond is a floating-rate bond whose coupon is swapped out to fixed rate.

The existence of the basis enables us to quantify the theoretical gain for the arbitrageur. As with other basis-type trades, typified by the government bond basis, the existence of a non–zero basis implies a risk-free arbitrage opportunity. If the basis is non–zero, a trader can put on a credit-risk-free arbitrage trade across the cash and synthetic markets. The two scenarios are:

❑ *Positive basis:* sell the cash bond and sell protection on that bond.
❑ *Negative basis:* buy the bond and buy protection using a CDS. In this trade, the investor has the value of the delivery option (we assume a physically settled CDS).

The first trade requires short-covering in the repo market, which exposes the investor to funding risks if the bond goes special. The latter trade is easier to implement, as there are no short-cover issues to consider, but it must be funded on the balance sheet. Therefore, the investor's funding costs will also impact the profitability of the trade. If it is sub-Libor, the trade should look attractive, and the investor will profit by the amount of the basis; if the funding cost is above Libor, it must be below the negative basis value for the trade to work. Because the basis trade for a negative basis is easier to implement, however, negative basis values rarely stay negative for long, and revert to positive once arbitrageurs get to work.

The basis can also be used to identify ways to enhance portfolio returns for a fund manager who is able to switch from cash to synthetic markets and vice versa. As the basis moves, it indicates which sector is experiencing widening spreads, into which fund managers can switch. Alternatively, a fund manager who has a view on which corporate sectors are likely to experience significant moves in the basis can move into that sector and undertake a basis trade to benefit from this move.

We examine these issues further in Chapter 6.

Summary

From this study of the credit default swap basis, we can conclude that the CDS market is very liquid and very closely correlated to the movements of the cash bond market. Although the theoretical argument can be made, using the no-arbitrage principle, that the CDS premium must equal the asset-swap premium, market observation tells us that a non–zero credit default swap bond basis always exists between the CDS and asset-swap markets. A non–zero basis arises from the influence of a number of technical and market factors, the impact of which varies with market conditions.

The basis moves closely with the markets as a whole. The relationship between the synthetic and cash markets, which is measured by the basis, is a two-way one, and the synthetic market will often lead the cash market. This experience, which mirrors the relationship in the interest-rate market between cash bonds and interest-rate derivatives, is a clear indicator of the liquid market that now prevails in credit default swaps.

References

Anson, M., F. Fabozzi, M. Choudhry, and Ren-Raw Chen. 2004. *Credit derivatives: Instruments and applications.* Hoboken, NJ: John Wiley & Sons.

Bank of England. 1997. Review of the gilt repo market. *Quarterly Bulletin* (February).

Bomfim, A. 2002. Credit derivatives and their potential to synthesize riskless assets. *Journal of Fixed Income* 12 (3) (December): 6–16.

Choudhry, M., 2001. Some issues in the asset-swap pricing of credit default swaps. *Derivatives Week*, Euromoney Institutional Investor PLC (December 2).

———. 2002. Combining securitisation and trading in credit derivatives: An analysis of the managed synthetic collateralised debt obligation. In *Euromoney debt capital markets handbook 2002.* London: Euromoney Publications.

Fabozzi, F., and L. Goodman, eds. 2001. *Investing in collateralised debt obligations.* New Hope, PA: FJF Associates.

Tolk, J. 2001. Understanding the risks in credit default swaps. *Moody's Special Report* (March 16).

CHAPTER 4

Supply and Demand and the Credit Default Swap Basis

I n this chapter, we consider the impact of supply and demand across both the cash and synthetic markets and their impact on the basis. This serves to further illustrate the interaction between the two markets. We then discuss why the traditional asset-swap (ASW) method of measuring the basis may no longer be preferred, a theme explored to greater depth in Chapter 5.

One of the factors that impact the basis is supply and demand, in both cash and synthetic markets. For many reference names, there is greater liquidity in the synthetic market than in the cash market, which would tend to influence the basis into negative territory, but other factors push the basis the other way (see previous chapter). With structured finance assets such as asset-backed securities (ABS), though, supply in the cash market is a key factor, and has been responsible for a negative basis over a longer time period than observed in conventional bond markets.

Supply and Demand

The bonds we will consider in this illustration are all examples of residential mortgage-backed securities (RMBS)—in fact, a

TABLE 4.1 *Securities used in illustration, showing CDS and cash market prices, September 21, 2004*

BOND	AMOUNT ISSUED ($MM)	CDS SPREAD
ACCR 2004-3 2M7	7.665	335
CWL 2004-6 B	46.0	340
NCHET 2004-2 M9	19.374	345

special class of RMBS known as Home Equity.[1] We show three of these bonds in **TABLE 4.1**, with rate spreads as of September 2004.

All three bonds were part of new issues, for first settlement in September 2004. The mezzanine tranches were in high demand at time of issue. Under conventional circumstances, the CDS price for these securities would be expected to lie above the Note yield. But in fact, the opposite is true, as the market quotes shown in Table 4.1 indicate. This reflects the lack of supply of these bonds in the market, such that investors are forced to access them in the synthetic market.

The small size of these Note tranches is a key reason behind the low availability of paper. We see that only $7.6 million of the ACCR bond is available, a very low figure in any securitization. The entire securitization itself is a large issue, as we see from **FIGURE 4.1**. This shows the Bloomberg DES page

---

1. For further information on Home Equity securities, see Fabozzi (2004). For further detail on securitization generally, ABS, and mortgage-backed securities (MBS), see Choudhry (2004a).

LIBOR SPREAD ON NOTE	CUSIP NUMBER	INTEREST FREQUENCY
350	004375BX8	Monthly on 25th
375	126673BL5	Monthly on 25th
400	64352VGJ4	Monthly on 25th

FIGURE 4.1 *Bloomberg screen DES for ACCR Home Equity securitization transaction*

```
                                                    Mtge    DES
       50<Go> for alternate group.
   Bloomberg            GROUP  DESCRIPTION            Page 2 of 3
   ABS                  ACCR 2004-3  Group-4: 30YR/MIX/G2G3    last  8/31/04
                        Issuer: ACCREDITED MORTGAGE LOAN TRUST       0 Prospectus
   Series 2004-3                               Assumed:   HOMEEQ 6.36 N

                        GROUP - ASSUMED         PSA-GROUP-CPR HOMEEQ 6.25 N
                       USD     766,436,984   1mo    -     -     -     -
          ACTUAL       Net         6.357%    3mo    -     -     -     -
                       WAC         6.859%    6mo    -     -     -     -
       COLLATERAL      WAM  29:8   356 mo    12mo   -     -     -     -
                       AGE   0:1     1 mo    Life   -     -     -     -
          NOT          1st paymt   9/25/04
                       1st settle  8/26/04   Monthly PAYMENT
       AVAILABLE       px3.00 PPS  8/17/04   pays 25th day
                       PAC   0%  SUP   0%    0 day delay      6) Lead Mgr: LB
                       Dated       8/26/04   accrues ACT/360  7) Trustee:  DBT
```

for the transaction, which is called Accredited Mortgage Loan Trust. From this, we see that a total of $766,436,984 of Notes was issued as part of this deal, but the tranche in question—the Baa3/BBB-rated 2M7 piece—made up less than 1% of this total. Given this paucity of supply, the bond can be sourced more easily in the CDS market, but this carries with it a reduction in yield spread, associated with the greater demand over supply.[2]

We observe similar characteristics for the two other bonds in our sample. The Countrywide Asset-Backed Certificates transaction is made up of a total of $4.426 billion in 12 different tranches; the mezzanine tranche rated Baa3/BBB was issued in size of only $46 million. The total size of the New Century Home Equity Loan Trust deal was $1.937 billion, while the particular mezzanine tranche we are interested in was issued in size of only 1% of this total. This bond exhibits the widest spread in our small group, with the CDS trading at a premium of 55 basis points to the theoretical cash price.

CDS Mechanics

The CDS contracts written on these structured finance securities have minor differences in their terms compared to vanilla single-name CDS instruments. This includes the following:

❑ A premium payment set to match the payment date of the cash bond, in this case a monthly payment on the 25th of each month. The standard CDS payment terms are quarterly in arrears.

❑ In practice, an unfixed maturity date. The CDS written on these bonds is set to match their maturity. From **FIGURE 4.2**, we see that the ACCR 2M7 tranche has a weighted-average life (WAL) of 5.4 years. This is of course an estimate based on a specified prepayment rate, which is standard practice for all RMBS bonds. In reality, the bond may well pay off before or after 5.4 years. The CDS contract language specifies that the contract expires when the cash bond itself is fully paid off.

❑ The transaction undertaken by the investor for the CDS that references the ACCR 2M7 tranche was for a notional of

---

2. In effect, the cash market Note yield of 350 bps for this bond is a theoretical construct. Because the bond in effect cannot be purchased, as no paper is available, the cash market yield for this name cannot actually be earned by any investor.

FIGURE 4.2 *Bloomberg screen DES for 2M7 tranche of ACCR transaction, September 21, 2004*

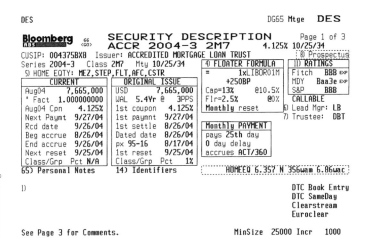

$10 million. This is more than the actual amount in existence of the physical bond. Hence, it is standard practice for all structured finance CDS contracts to always be cash-settled instruments.

By setting the terms in this way, investors are able to access these types of names and asset classes where the cash market bond is no longer available to them, by selling protection on the bond tranches using a CDS.

The CDS market maker that is the counterparty to the CDS investor may gain from acting in this business in the following ways:

❑ Buying protection on this class of assets releases economic capital that can be invested in higher-yielding assets elsewhere.

❑ It may be able to find similar assets in the cash market that yield a higher spread than the CDS protection it is paying for.

❑ It can treat this business as trading activity—CDS market making—and seek to gain a trading profit.

Irrespective of the motivation of the investor and the CDS counterparty to these trades, this business illustrates the contribution to market liquidity of credit derivatives, as well as the impact of supply and demand on reversing the market convention of a positive basis.

A Different Basis Measure

The difference between the CDS and the ASW price, the CDS basis, was given in the previous chapter as

credit default spread (D) – the asset-swap spread (S).[3]

Where $D - S > 0$, we have a *positive basis*. A positive basis occurs when the credit derivative trades higher than the asset-swap price, and is the norm. Where $D - S < 0$, we have a *negative basis*. This describes where the credit derivative trades tighter than the cash bond asset-swap spread. It is more unusual to see this for any length of time. On balance, the net impact of all the factors that drive the basis serves to make it positive. In essence, this is because the seller of protection on a standard CDS contract is affording a greater level of protection on the reference name than a cash investor in a bond issued by that reference name.

The ASW method, however, gives a different measure for the basis than other spread measures. **FIGURE 4.3** shows Bloomberg screen ASW for the British Telecom 8.125% 2010 bond, as of December 1, 2005. This indicates an asset-swap spread of 74.0

---

3. At this stage, we may state the formal definition of the credit default swap–bond basis as being the difference between the credit default spread and the par bond floating-rate spread of the same reference asset, the latter as expressed for an asset swap on the bond.

FIGURE 4.3   *Bloomberg screen ASW, asset-swap spread for British Telecom bond as of December 1, 2005*

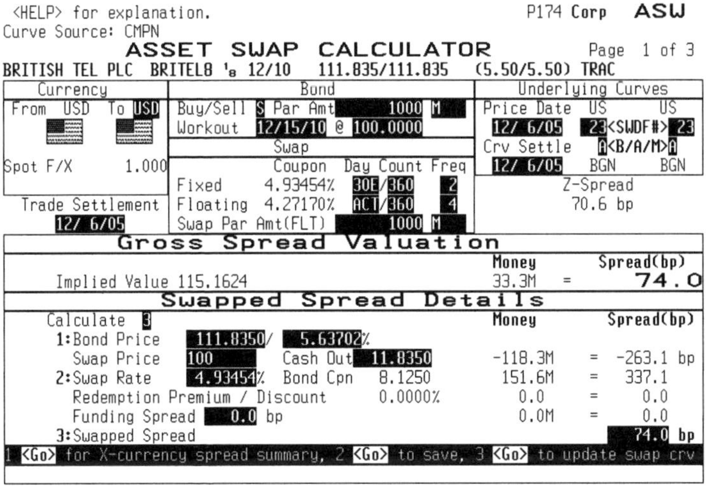

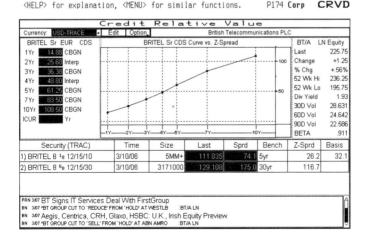

FIGURE 4.4   *Bloomberg screen CRVD, CDS curve versus Z-spread for British Telecom bond as of December 1, 2005*

Source: Bloomberg

Source: Bloomberg

basis points. **FIGURE 4.4** shows screen CRVD for the British Telecom reference name, which lists the ASW spread as well as CDS prices for that entity. We see that the price for this bond in the CDS market is 61.25 basis points; this is the 5-year CDS price for British Telecom, and would appear to be the best price to compare because the bond in question is a 5-year bond. From these two values, it is a simple calculation to determine the basis as defined above, which would be –12.75 basis points. The value shown in Figure 4.4, however, is 32.1 basis points, a positive value. This is because screen CRVD measures the basis relative to the bond *Z-spread*, which is shown as 26.2 basis points and lies below the CDS curve (also shown in Figure 4.4).

So, we note that either the asset-swap spread or the Z-spread can be used in the basis calculation. Each gives a different measure of the basis. Although market practitioners appear to use the latter as often as the former, it is important to be aware of exactly what is being measured, so that relative analysis remains accurate. We explore this issue in the next chapter.

References

Choudhry, M. 2001. Some issues in the asset-swap pricing of credit default swaps. *Derivatives Week* (December 2).

———. 2004a. *Structured credit products: Credit derivatives and synthetic securitisation.* Singapore: John Wiley & Sons.

———. 2004b. The credit default swap basis: Analysing the relationship between cash and synthetic markets. *Journal of Derivatives Use, Trading and Regulation 10 (1)* (June): 9–26.

Fabozzi, F., ed. 2004. *The handbook of fixed income securities,* 7th ed. New York: McGraw-Hill.

CHAPTER 5

The CDS Basis II:
Further Analysis of the Cash and Synthetic Credit Market Differential

In the previous chapter, we described the traditional method of calculating the credit default swap (CDS) basis. For accurate analysis, this is now regarded as misleading, especially when bond prices are trading above or below par. Investors often require more effective measures of the basis. In this chapter, we assess why the common measure of the basis is inappropriate in certain cases, before considering alternative measures that should better suit investors' purposes. We conclude that an adjusted Z-spread, based on default probabilities implied by credit default swap prices, is the best measure to use when calculating the basis.

Basis and Relative Value

A basis exists in every market where cash and derivatives on the cash are traded. The cash-CDS basis is the difference in value between the CDS market and the cash bond market. The existence of a non–zero basis implies potential trading gains of either of the following:

❏ *Negative basis:* where there is a relatively low spread in the CDS market and a higher spread for the cash bond. That is, in relative terms, the bond is cheap and the CDS is dear. In a negative basis strategy, which is effected by buying the cash bond and buying protection on the same name, the trader aims to earn a risk-free return by buying and selling identical credit risk but across two different markets.

❏ *Positive basis:* effected by selling the cash bond and selling CDS protection on the same name, with the aim of exploiting a relatively low value CDS price and a low spread (high price) bond value.

For reasons of transparency and accessibility, investors require a measurement of value that is relative to Libor. With a CDS contract, there is only one measure of value, the "spread," and so no uncertainty as to which measure is the correct one. With cash bonds, however, the quoted price can be translated into more than one Libor spread—namely, the interpolated spread, asset-swap spread (ASW), yield-to-maturity spread over swaps, and the Z-spread. The choice of which Libor spread to use therefore becomes central to the issue of basis measurement.

Basis Spread Measures

A wide range of factors drives the basis. These factors were described in detail in Chapter 3. The existence of a non–zero basis has implications for investment strategy. For instance, when the basis is negative, investors may prefer to hold the cash bond; whereas if—for liquidity, supply, or other reasons—the basis is positive, the investor may wish to hold the asset synthetically, by selling protection using a credit default swap. Another approach is to arbitrage between the cash and synthetic markets, in the case of a negative basis by buying the cash bond and shorting it synthetically by buying protection in the CDS market. Investors have a range of spreads to use when performing their relative value analysis.

Because the synthetic market in credit is often viewed to be a reliable indicator of the cash market in credit, it is important for all market participants to be familiar with the two-way relationship between the two markets. The relationship is represented by the credit default swap basis: a measure of the difference in price and value between the cash and synthetic credit markets. An accurate measure of the basis is vital for an effective assessment of the relationship between the two markets to be made.

ASW Spread

The potential to create an opportunity for arbitrage trading between the cash and synthetic markets means that often the basis is actually quite small in size. This infrequency of opportunity, however, means that it is vital to obtain an accurate measure. The traditional method used to calculate the basis given by equation (3.1) in Chapter 3 can be regarded as being of sufficient accuracy only if the following conditions are satisfied:

- ❑ The CDS and bond are of matching maturities;
- ❑ For many reference names, both instruments carry a similar level of subordination.

The conventional approach for analyzing an asset swap uses the bond's yield-to-maturity (YTM) in calculating the spread. The assumptions implicit in the YTM calculation also make this spread problematic for relative analysis.

The most critical issue, however, is the nature of the construction of the asset-swap structure itself: the need for the cash bond price to be priced at or very near to par. Most corporate bonds trade significantly away from par, thus rendering the par asset-swap price an inaccurate measure of their credit risk. The standard asset swap is constructed as a par product; hence, if the bond being asset-swapped is trading above par, then the swap price will overestimate the level of credit risk. If the bond is trading below par, the asset swap will underestimate the credit risk associated with the bond. We see, then, that using the CDS-ASW method will provide an unreliable measure of the basis. We therefore need to use another methodology for measuring the basis.

Z-Spread

A commonly used alternative to the ASW spread is the Z-spread. The Z-spread uses the zero-coupon yield curve to calculate spread, so in theory is a more effective spread to use. The zero-coupon curve used in the calculation is derived from the interest-rate swap curve. Put simply, the Z-spread is the basis-point spread that would need to be added to the implied spot yield curve such that the discounted cash flows of a bond are equal to its present value (its current market price). Each bond cash flow is discounted by the relevant spot rate for its maturity term. How does this differ from the conventional asset-swap spread? Essentially, in its use of zero-coupon rates when assigning a value to a bond. Each cash flow is discounted using its own particular zero-coupon rate. A bond's price at any time can be taken to be the market's value of the bond's cash flows. Using the Z-spread, we can quantify what the swap market thinks of this value—that is, by how much the conventional spread differs from the Z-spread. Both spreads can be viewed as the coupon of a swap market annuity of equivalent credit risk of the bond being valued.

The Z-spread was described in detail in Chapter 2.

In practice, the Z-spread, especially for shorter-dated bonds and for higher-credit-quality bonds, does not differ greatly from the conventional asset-swap spread. The Z-spread is usually the higher spread of the two, following the logic of spot rates, but not always. If it differs greatly, then the bond can be considered to be mispriced.

Critique of the Z-Spread

Although the Z-spread is an improved value to use when calculating the basis compared to the ASW spread, it is not a direct comparison with a CDS premium. This is because it does not allow for probability of default—or, more specifically, timing of default. The Z-spread uses the correct zero-coupon rates to discount each bond cash flow, but it does not reflect the fact that, as coupons are received over time, each cash flow will carry a different level of credit risk. In fact, each cash flow will represent different levels of credit risk.

Given that a corporate bond that pays a spread over Treasuries or Libor must, by definition, be assumed to carry credit risk, we need to incorporate a probability of default factor if we compare its value to that of the same-name CDS. If the bond defaults, investors expect to receive a proportion of their holding back; this amount is given by the recovery rate. If the probability of default is p, then investors will receive the recovery rate amount after default. Prior to this, they will receive $(1 - p)$. To gain an accurate measure of the basis therefore, we should incorporate this probability of default factor.

Adjusted Z-Spread

For the most accurate measure of the basis when undertaking relative value strategy, investors should employ the adjusted Z-spread, sometimes known as the C-spread. With this methodology, cash flows are adjusted by their probability of being paid. Because the default probability will alter over time, a static value cannot be used, so the calculation is done using a binomial approach, with the relevant default probability for each cash-flow pay date. An adjusted Z-spread can be calculated by either converting the bond price to a CDS-equivalent price, or converting a CDS spread to a bond-equivalent price. This is then subtracted from the CDS spread to give the adjusted basis.

Analyzing the Basis

We wish to formulate a framework by which we can "price" the basis, in effect a more effective method to analyze the basis beyond the first-generation principles outlined in Choudhry (2004). This requires that we understand the behavior and characteristics of the CDS as a hedging instrument.

Simplified Approach

All else being equal, under equation (3.1), we would expect the basis to be negative, due to the financing costs associated with the cash bond position. In practice, as we saw in Chapter 3, a

FIGURE 5.1 *CDS convexity*

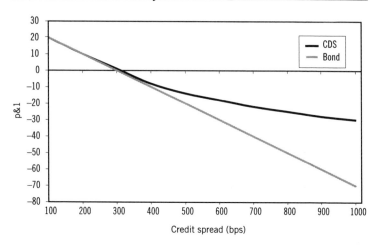

wide range of technical and market factors drives the basis, and it is more common to observe a positive basis. When considering the basis, the coupon level on the cash bond is key to the analysis and also drives the basis. Bonds will trade above par when their coupon is high relative to current interest rates (given by swap rates); they trade below par when the opposite occurs. When above par, asset-swap spreads should be expected to lie above CDS premiums and so drive the basis downward, and vice versa when the bond price is below par. In addition, the CDS exhibits convexity, since the profit and loss on a CDS position does not move in direct proportion to the change in the credit spread. This is illustrated in **FIGURE 5.1**. Because this is not the case for asset-swap values, especially at higher credit spreads, we take this into account when pricing the basis.

To value the basis, then, we want to account for the instruments' convexity. We use the instruments' duration in this analysis, a value required if calculating the position p&l. An effective approximation of CDS duration is given by

$$D_{CDS} = \frac{1 - e^{-\left(rs + \frac{P_{CDS}}{LR}\right) \times M}}{rs + \dfrac{P_{CDS}}{LR}}, \qquad (5.1)$$

where

rs is swap rate

P_{CDS} is CDS margin

M is maturity (years)

LR is loss rate.

We noted there are two approaches to equate CDS premiums with bond prices. One approach is to value the bond using CDS reference prices. To do this, we need to transform the latter into a synthetic bond, and then use this synthetic bond value to calculate the basis. This produces more of a "like-for-like" spread that we can then compare to the cash spread.

We require therefore the asset-swap spread, obtained from the CDS duration as follows:

$$ASW = CDS \times \frac{D_{CDS}}{D_{Swap}} + (C - rs) \times \left(1 - \frac{D_{CDS}}{D_{Swap}}\right), \qquad (5.2)$$

where

CDS is CDS spread

C is coupon.

In other words, we can calculate the asset-swap spread directly from the CDS of similar maturity. The simplified model shown above is straightforward to calculate, and focuses on the two main factors that make basis calculation problematic: the convexity effects of CDSs compared to bonds, and the coupon effects of bonds being priced away from par. With the former, as CDS spreads widen, their duration decreases, so that bond spreads narrow relative to CDS spreads. With the latter, the higher the coupon relative to market rates (given by the swap rate for the same maturity), the wider will be the asset-swap spread relative to CDSs.

Unfortunately, the simple model is not practical because coupons are not continuously compounded and so require adjustment. Also, there is not always a bond and CDS of near-similar maturities to use in comparison. We therefore adopt another approach.

Pricing the Basis

Given the shortcomings of the methods described up to now, we wish to apply a technique that enables us to calculate the basis more effectively, on a more "like-for-like" level. Remember, we have two sources of credit-risk pricing: the cash bond yield and the CDS premium. When making the comparison between the two markets, we need to adjust one before comparing to the other, hence the name "adjusted basis" or "adjusted Z-spread." To calculate the basis, then, we can do one of the following:

- ❑ Calculate the cash bond spread given by the CDS term structure; that is, price the bond according to the CDS curve and compare this spread to the bond market spread; or

- ❑ Calculate the CDS price given by the bond yield curve; that is, price the CDS on the bond curve and then compare it to the CDS market price.

In theory, the basis should be the same whichever approach is used.

Either approach can be adopted in principle, although the first approach is more problematic because the bond price (yield) does not make explicit which term default probability it is that is being priced. Under the latter approach, we can use the CDS term structure to build a default probability curve. We look at both approaches in the next section; first, we examine the theoretical background.

General Pricing Framework

We need to set first the relationships for CDS and bond pricing. With a CDS, the contract is terminated on occurrence of a credit event, with settlement taking place upon payment of the accrued premium.

If

$$D(t) = \sum_i \left(T_i - T_{i-1}\right) \times P\left(T_i\right) \qquad (5.3)$$

is the duration of an interest-rate swap of maturity t, and T_i is the fixed-rate payment dates, then we therefore write the duration of the CDS contract at the termination date as

$$D_{\min}(t) = \sum_{(i)} \left(\min\left(t, T_i\right) - \min\left(t, T_{i-1}\right)\right) \times P\left(t, T_i\right), \quad (5.4)$$

where

$P(t)$ is the price of a zero-coupon risk-free bond of maturity t
T is the maturity date of both CDS and cash bond.

The net present value (NPV) of the CDS fixed-rate premiums is given by

$$S(t)\, E_\tau\left[D_{\min}(\tau)\right] = S(t) \times \left[\int_0^T D_{\min}(t)\, f_\tau(t)\, dt + Q(\tau > T)\, D(T)\right],$$

$$(5.5)$$

where

$S(t)$ is the credit spread for contract of maturity t
τ is the date of the credit event
f_τ is the unconditional rate of default at any given time
E_τ is the expectations operator at the date of the credit event.

We assume that a credit event is a default and vice versa. In fact, the NPV is given by multiplying the CDS spread by the CDS duration D_{CDS}.

The NPV of the protection payment on occurrence of credit event, which we denote as the CDS floating-rate payment, is given by

$$E_\tau\left[(1 - RR)\, P(\tau)_{\tau \leq T}\right] = (1 - RR) \int_0^T P(t)\, f_\tau(t)\, dt, \quad (5.6)$$

where

RR is the recovery rate, usually assumed to be 40%.
Note that $RR = 1 - LR$, where LR is the loss rate.

For bond valuation, we price the security as an asset-swap package. This is given by

$$S(T)D_{ASW}(T) = \sum_{i}(T_i - T_{i-1}) \times C$$

$$\times Q(\tau \leq T_i)P(T_i) + Q(\tau \leq T)P(T)$$

$$- \int_0^T RR \times P(t)f_\tau(t)\,dt, \qquad (5.7)$$

where

D_{ASW} is the duration of the interest-rate swap in an asset-swap package

C is the coupon of the fixed-rate bond in the asset-swap package

Q is the probability of survival.

To reiterate, we have two ways to compute the adjusted basis: we can price the CDS using the bond curve, or price the bond on the CDS curve.

If we wish to price the CDS on the bond curve, we use equation (5.6) above to obtain the probability density f_τ that gives us the correct market spreads for a set of asset swaps. We then use this density when calculating the CDS price using equation (5.7) above, which gives us a CDS spread based on the bond price. To price the bond on the CDS curve, we use the CDS price formula to find the probability density f_τ that gives us the correct market spreads for a set of CDS prices. We use this density in the bond price formula (5.7), which gives us a CDS-based bond asset-swap spread.

From the above, it can be shown that

$$S_{ASW}(T)D(T) = (C - r) \times (D(T) - D_{CDS}(T)) + S_{CDS}(T)D_{CDS}(T), \qquad (5.8)$$

where r is the swap rate corresponding to maturity date T.

The expression (5.8) relates two significant factors driving the basis, namely:

❏ The coupon, or the change in asset-swap spread given change in CDS spread, bond coupon, and swap rate; and

❏ The convexity, a function of the difference between D_{CDS} and D_{ASW}.

In the next section, we describe a practical market approach to calculating the adjusted basis.

Adjusted Basis Calculation

We look now at pricing the CDS on the bond-equivalent convention—that is, converting the CDS price to a CDS-equivalent bond spread. This approach reduces uncertainty, as there is a directly observable credit curve, the CDS curve, to which we can attach specific default probabilities. The CDS curve for a large number of reference names is liquid across the term structure from 1 through to 10, 15, and often 20 years. This is not the case with a corporate bond curve.[1]

The basis measure calculated using this method is known as the adjusted basis. It is given by

$$\text{adjusted basis} = \text{adjusted CDS spread} - \text{Z-spread}. \quad (5.9)$$

The Z-spread is the same measure described earlier in this chapter—that is, the actual Z-spread of the cash bond in question. Instead of comparing it to a market CDS premium, though, we compare it to the CDS-equivalent spread of the traded bond. The adjusted CDS spread is known as the adjusted Z-spread, CDS spread, or C-spread. The adjusted basis is the difference between these two spreads.

The adjusted CDS spread is calculated by applying CDS market default probabilities to the cash bond in question. In other words, it gives a hypothetical price for the actual bond. This price is not related to the actual market price, but should, unless the

---

1. Unless the corporate issuer in question has a continuous debt program, that means it has issued bonds at regular (say 6-month) intervals across the entire term structure.

latter is significantly mispriced, be close to it. It is a function of the default probabilities implied by the CDS curve, the assumed recovery rate, and the bond's cash flows. Once calculated, the adjusted CDS spread is used to obtain the basis.

To calculate the adjusted CDS spread, we carry out the following:

❑ Plot a term structure of credit rates using CDS quotes from the market. The quotes will all be single-name CDS prices for the reference credit in question. For the greatest accuracy, we use as many CDS prices as possible (from the 6-month to the 20-year maturity, at 6-month intervals where possible), although the number of quotes will depend on the liquidity of the name.

❑ From the credit curve, we derive a cumulative default probability curve. This is used together with the value for the recovery rate to construct a survival curve by bootstrapping default probabilities.

❑ The survival curve is used to price the bond in line with a binomial tree model. This is shown in **FIGURE 5.2**, where we see that the bond's cash flow of coupon and principal follows a binomial path of payment if no default or payment of recovery amount RR in event of default. Each cash flow is discounted at the swap rate relevant to that term; the discounting is weighted according to the relevant term default probability. The sum of these probability-weighted discounted cash flows is the bond's hypothetical price. It represents the price of the CDS if it traded as a bond, in effect the price of a credit-linked note or funded CDS. For simplicity, the cash flow at each payment date can be discounted at a single market rate such as the swap rate or Libor rate as well. The aggregate of these cash flows, the hypothetical bond price, will differ from the observed market price.

❑ The adjusted CDS spread is the spread above (or below) the swap curve that equates the bond's observed market price to its hypothetical price calculated above.

The adjusted CDS spread can be viewed as the Z-spread of the bond at its hypothetical price. Comparing it to the actual

FIGURE **5.2** *Calculating the bond hypothetical price using
implied default probabilities*

C% 1.5-year bond

Binomial tree of probabilty-weighted discounted cash-flow method to calculate
hypothetical bond price

The probability of default at each time period is given as p_i.

Probability is conditional on survival at time $i - 1$.

Discount rate is relevant tenor swap rate for each cash flow or maturity date
swap rate for all cash flows.

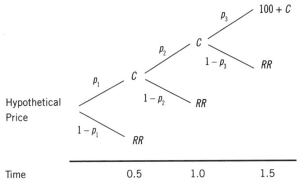

Z-spread, then, gives us a like-for-like comparison and a more
robust measure of the basis.

In other words, we produce an adjusted Z-spread based on
CDS prices, and compare it to the Z-spread of the bond at its
actual market price. We have still compared the synthetic asset
price to the cash asset price, as given originally in equation (3.1)
in Chapter 3, but the comparison is now a logical one.

The alternative approach we suggested earlier of adjusting a
bond spread into an equivalent CDS spread can also be followed,
but suffers from a paucity of observable market data. We would
need a sufficient number of bonds with maturities from the short
to the long end of the curve, and this is available only from large
issuers with continuous programs, such as Ford. On the other
hand, as we noted earlier, the CDS market can be used to plot a

FIGURE 5.3 *Illustrating the hypothetical bond price calculation based on CDS-implied default probability*

ABC PLC	
6% Nov 2008 bond	USD bond
Price	102.47
8-Nov-05	

Hypothetical price	The price obtained using default probabilities implied by CDS prices
	Given by:
	(1) Multiplying each bond cash flow by the probability of receiving that cash flow
	(2) Discounting each cash flow by the relevant swap curve discount factor to obtain present value
	(3) Aggregating discounted cash flows

ABC PLC CDS prices	Mid-prices general screen quote			
Term	1	3	5	10
Spread bps	12	21	30	41

	Mid-prices specific quotes					
	0.5	1	1.5	2	2.5	3
	5	12	14	17	19	21

Default probability relationship

   CDS spread = Default probability × (1 − RR) OR Default probability × LR

Default probability	= CDS spread / LR
	= 0.0021 / 0.6
	= 0.0035
Date of cash flow	8-Nov-08
Maturity	3 years

Cash flows	0.5	1	1.5	2	2.5	3	
	3	3	3	3	3	103	= 118

Default probability	0.0035
Survival probability	1 − Default probability
	= 0.9965
Loss rate	1 − RR
	= 60%
Swap rate	4.90
	Discount factor = $1/(1 + 3yr\ swap\ rate)^3$
	0.86631041
Hypothetical price	[Bond cash flow × Survival probability + RR
	× Default probability] × Discount factor
	101.8680556

credit curve for many more reference names out to the 20-year end of the curve or even beyond.

Illustration

We illustrate the technique with an example using a hypothetical corporate bond, the ABC PLC 6% of 2008. This is shown in **FIGURE 5.3**. We set it so that the ABC PLC bond has exactly 3 years to maturity, and we discount the cash flows using only the 3-year rate, rather than each cash flow at its own specific term discount rate. This is just to simplify the calculation. If we have fractions in the remaining time to maturity, we use the exact time period (in years) to adjust the default probabilities.

The market price of the bond is $102.47. The hypothetical price is $101.87. The Z-spread of the bond at its market price is 14 basis points. To calculate the adjusted Z-spread, we apply the process we described earlier in this chapter; this gives us an adjusted Z-spread, or hypothetical price Z-spread, of 19.9 basis points. This is near to the CDS spread of 21 basis points.

The adjusted basis is therefore

$$\text{adjusted Z-spread} - \text{Z-spread},$$

which is $19.9 - 14$, or 5.9 basis points. Compare this to the conventional basis, which is

$$\text{CDS price} - \text{ASW spread},$$

which is $21 - 23.12$, or -2.12 basis points.

So the true basis is, in this example, not negative but positive. Further analysis of the kind we have undertaken would have argued against a basis trade that might have looked attractive due to the negative basis indicating potential value.

Market Observation

The foregoing highlights some of the issues involved in measuring the basis. Irrespective of the calculation method employed,

FIGURE 5.4 *Selected telecoms corporate name, cash-CDS basis, 2003–2005*

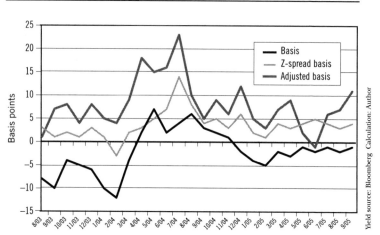

the one certainty is that corporate names in cash and synthetic markets do trade out of line; the basis is driven across positive and negative ranges due to the impact of a diverse range of technical, structural, and market factors (see Chapter 3). Of course, any basis value that is not zero implies potential value in arbitrage trades in that reference name, be it buying or selling the basis.

The conventional situation is a positive basis, as a negative basis implies a risk-free arbitrage profit is available. Market observation suggests that a negative basis is more common than might be expected, however. **FIGURE 5.4** shows the basis—measured in each of the three ways we have highlighted—for a selected corporate name in the telecoms sector for the period August 2003 to September 2005. There is occasional relatively wide divergence between the measures, but all measures show the move from positive to negative territory and then back again.

Summary

The high level of liquidity now available in synthetic credit markets, which now encompass structured finance securities as well corporate names, has resulted in basis trading's becoming an important sector in relative value trading. Because value in the cash market can be measured in a number of ways as a spread to Libor, a key issue when calculating the basis is which Libor spread measure to use. This is not an issue for the CDS leg of the equation, as there is only one, unambiguous value for a CDS.

The most common spread measure is the asset-swap spread. As a par product, this becomes an inaccurate measure of credit risk if the bond itself is trading away from par. The Z-spread, while a more appropriate measure of value than the ASW spread, also suffers from not incorporating any element of default probability in its calculation.

We observed that the basis is driven by coupon and convexity issues, which we formalized in a relationship among the spread of the bond, its coupon, and the respective durations of the bond and CDS. We determined that the adjusted Z-spread was the most effective measure of the cash market to use when measuring the basis. The approach to calculate this creates a hypothetical bond price from default-probability-weighted discounted cash flows. Using this measure enables us to compare like-for-like, and so arrive at a more logical value for the basis. This should enable investors to better analyze potential value in relative value trades.

References

Choudhry, M. 2004. *Structured credit products: Credit derivatives and synthetic securitisation*. Singapore: John Wiley & Sons.

CHAPTER 6

Trading the CDS Basis: Illustrating Positive and Negative Basis Arbitrage Trades

T he foregoing chapters have introduced and described the cash–synthetic credit market basis, which we have chosen to call the credit default swap (CDS) basis. A basis exists in any market where cash and derivative forms of the same asset are traded. We have seen how, given that the derivative represents the cash asset in underlying form, there is a close relationship between the two types, which manifests itself in the basis and its magnitude. Fluctuations in the basis give rise to arbitrage trading opportunities between the two forms of the asset. This has proved the case in a more recent market, that of credit derivatives.[1]

In Chapter 2, we summarized the logic behind the no-arbitrage theory of pricing credit default swaps, which suggests that the premium of a CDS should be equal to an asset-swap (ASW) spread for the same reference name. There are a number of reasons why this is not the case, described in Chapter 3, and in practice a non–zero basis exists for all reference names in the credit markets. The existence of a non–zero basis implies potential arbitrage gains that can be made if trading in both the cash and derivatives markets simultaneously.

---

1. The trades described here are not pure arbitrage trades, because they are not completely risk free. This is discussed in the section on hedging and risk.

In this chapter, we describe trading the basis, with real-world examples given of such trades, illustrating the positive basis trade and the negative basis trade.

Relative Value and Trading the Basis

The introduction of credit derivatives into the financial markets has provided a new asset class for investors in credit-risky assets. That credit derivatives, particularly credit default swaps, can be traded in a liquid market in a wide range of names provides investors and other market participants with an additional measure of relative value across the cash and synthetic markets. The existence of a non–zero basis, either positive or negative, can act as a powerful indicator of value in either or both markets. In addition, during an economic boom period or time of general business confidence, when corporate credit spreads are tight, investors look to new opportunities to meet target rates of return or realize value. Exploiting mispricing in cash and synthetic markets, through basis arbitrage trading, is one such opportunity.

As we noted in passing in Chapter 3, there are two types of basis trade:

❏ *Negative basis* trade: this position is defined as buying the bond and buying protection on the same reference name. It is generally put on if the CDS spread[2] is relatively low compared to where it has been, and if the cash bond spread is relatively high. The objective of a negative basis trade is to earn a credit-risk-free return by buying and selling the cash and the synthetic. In a negative basis trade, the cash bond is viewed as cheap and the CDS as dear.

❏ *Positive basis* trade: this is where the arbitrageur will sell

---

2. Throughout this book, we have referred to the CDS "spread" when a more accurate term would be "premium" or "fee." The CDS spread is not a spread over anything, but more simply a fixed price quoted in basis points. However, market common practice is to refer to the CDS "spread" in the same way as we refer to an asset-swap spread, which is a spread over Libor, so we continue the practice here.

the bond and sell CDS protection on the same name, to exploit a price differential that is brought about by a relatively high CDS price and a relatively low cash bond spread.

As we discussed in Chapters 3 and 5, there is more than one way to measure the basis. Whichever approach we employ, in essence we are comparing a CDS premium to a spread over Libor, so all analysis is undertaken relative to Libor. Put simply, we wish to earn a spread pickup on our trade, so the largest possible spread gain will generate the largest profit. There are other considerations as well, which can include the following:

❑ Extent of credit-risk premium received and/or earned
❑ Any impact of the "cheapest-to-deliver" option for the protection buyer
❑ Impact of funding cost of the cash asset
❑ The effect of basis trades in reference names that trade at sub-Libor in the cash market[3]
❑ The relative levels of liquidity in the cash and synthetic market
❑ The effectiveness of the trade hedge

The last point we mention is very important. To be a pure arbitrage, the basis package must hedge both credit risk and interest-rate risk. For large-size trades, spread risk may also need to be hedged.[4] Otherwise the trade will not be a pure risk-free one, and the final return on it will be influenced by (at the time of inception) unknown factors.

As we noted in Chapter 3, the various factors that drive the basis tend to drive it to positive territory. In other words, a posi-

---

3. Names such as the World Bank or U.S. agency securities trade at sub-Libor in the cash market, so additional analysis is required to determine basis trade profit potential.

4. This is the risk that the relative spread of cash assets to Libor or the swap rate changes. One instrument that can be used to hedge spread risk is the LIFFE Swap-Note contract. For details of this derivative, see Choudhry (2004a, 2004b).

TABLE 6.1 *Average CDS and ASW spreads for selected industrial names during 2005*

CREDIT RATING	AVERAGE CDS PREMIUM	AVERAGE ASW SPREAD	DIFFERENCE (CDS – ASW)
AAA	22	12	10
AA	26	17	9
A	39	36	3
BBB	88	87	1
BB	256	247	9
Average	86.2	79.8	6.4

Spread source: Bloomberg

tive basis is the norm. **TABLE 6.1** shows the average CDS premium and ASW spread across the ratings categories for selected industrial names during 2005. For no set of names was a negative basis the average value. In other words, we should expect the CDS to trade higher than the cash. On average, CDS spreads are 6–7 basis points above ASW spreads. Overall, a negative basis is a good initial indicator that special factors are at work.

Factors Influencing the Basis Package

When constructing the basis trade, it is important that we compare like-for-like, and that we hedge the trade as effectively as possible. That is, we need to consider the most appropriate cash market spread against which to measure the CDS spread, and we need to also construct the hedge with care.

Measuring the Basis

The question of which cash market spread to use when measuring the basis is an important one. We saw in Chapter 5 that the different measures for the cash spread produce different values for the basis. The answer to this problem is not clear-cut; credit default swaps and cash bonds trade in different markets, with different market drivers, and a pure comparison may not actually be possible. We know that we need to select a Libor-based spread; the question is, which spread? As we noted earlier in this book, the CDS "spread" is not a spread at all, but rather, a fixed premium received quarterly by the protection seller. Although, in theory, the CDS spread and the ASW spread measure the credit risk of the reference name, other, more specific factors drive each of them, such that, in effect, they are actually measuring slightly different things. The CDS premium can be viewed as a pure credit-risk price—that is, it is the credit premium for the name. Although other factors will drive this premium, including supply and demand, at least as an unfunded instrument and par product, we know these considerations do not apply. We want to compare it therefore to the cash measure that is the most accurate measure of the reference entity's credit risk.

FIGURE 6.1 *Bloomberg page YAS for ThyssenKrupp AG 4.375% March 2015, as of March 13, 2006*

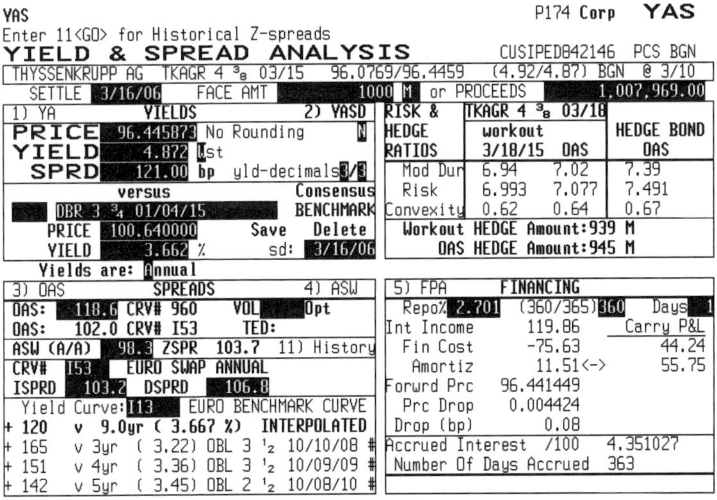

FIGURE 6.2 *Bloomberg page CRVD for ThyssenKrupp AG reference name, as of March 13, 2006*

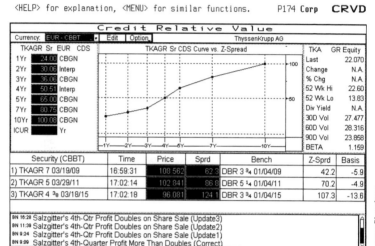

<HELP> for explanation, <MENU> for similar functions.   P174 **Corp   CRVD**

Security (CBBT)	Time	Price	Sprd	Bench	Z-Sprd	Basis
1) TKAGR 7 03/19/09	16:59:31	108.562	62.3	DBR 3 ¾ 01/04/09	42.2	-5.9
2) TKAGR 5 03/29/11	17:02:14	102.841	86.8	DBR 5 ¼ 01/04/11	70.2	-4.9
3) TKAGR 4 ⅜ 03/18/15	17:02:18	96.081	124.1	DBR 3 ¾ 01/04/15	107.3	-13.6

Source: Bloomberg

A cash bond spread can be measured in a number of ways, as we saw in Chapter 2. **FIGURE 6.1** shows the Bloomberg YAS page for a ThyssenKrupp AG issue, the 4.375% March 2015 bond. This shows the different bond spread measures that can be calculated. In a basis trade, it is the spread that is the best indicator of the reference name's credit-risk premium that we should, ideally, be comparing the CDS spread to. The CDS price is 93.7 basis points (bps), which is an interpolated spread based on the CDS curve. The CDS curve is shown on screen CRVD for this name, given in **FIGURE 6.2**.

We see from Figure 6.1 that for this name, we have
❑ an I-spread (ISPRD) of 103.2 bps;
❑ an asset-swap (ASW) spread of 98.3 bps; and
❑ a Z-spread (ZSPR) of 103.7 bps.

So, in other words, the Libor spread for this bond ranges from 98.3 bps to 103.7 bps. The spread to the government bond

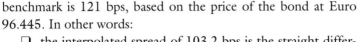

benchmark is 121 bps, based on the price of the bond at Euro
96.445. In other words:

❑ the interpolated spread of 103.2 bps is the straight difference between the bond gross redemption yield and Libor rate for
the same term;

❑ in an asset-swap package, the investor would receive Libor
+ 98.3 bps and an implied receipt of Euro 3.555 up front (as the
bond is priced below par) while paying the coupon of 4.375%
over the term of the deal; and

❑ the Z-spread of 103.7 bps represents the spread over and
above the interbank interest-rate swap curve that would equal the
bond's present value with its coupon and principal payments over
the term to maturity.

As we noted, for basis trading purposes, ideally we should
use the bond spread that best represents the credit premium payable for taking on the issuer's credit risk. There is no real "true"
answer, although in practice the ASW spread and the Z-spread
are the most commonly used. Note, however, as in this case, for
bonds that trade close to par, the various spread measures are
actually quite close.

As part of the analysis in a real-world situation, we should
also consider the actual return generated by a basis trade package. This takes into account market factors such as bid-offer
spread and funding costs. **TABLE 6.2** shows how we would
undertake this analysis at the closeout of the trade, be it after
1 month, 3 months, 1 year, or other target horizon. In this analysis, the total return of the trade is, unsurprisingly, a function
of the actual price of the bond at closeout. The actual result
is not known, as we do not know the price of the bond in the
future, at the time we put on the trade, hence the blank fields in
Table 6.2—we show this table to suggest how we should look
to perform the analysis. Later on in this chapter, we show some
real-world trade results.

TABLE 6.2 *Suggested return analysis for negative basis trade for 6-month trade horizon, ThyssenKrupp bond*

Cash-flow position versus par 1.00795

	PRICE TODAY: MARCH 13, 2006	PRICE AT CLOSEOUT	COST/GAIN
Bond mechanics			
Clean	96.445	x	$x - 96.445$
Accrued	4.35	ai	$ai - 4.35$
Dirty	100.795	$x + ai$	$(x + ai) - 100.795$
Fund bond position in repo (pay 1.00795%) 6-month EUR Libor 2.847%			-1.434
Interest-rate swap hedge: cash flow			
Pay fixed at 3.843%			-1.936
Receive 6-month Libor 2.847%			1.434
Total bond cash flows			
CDS mechanics			
Buy 9-year CDS protection at 93.7 bps			-0.4685
Total return			

The Hedge Construction

It is intuitively easy to view a basis package as a straight par-for-par trade of notionals. That is, we would buy (or sell) $10 million nominal of a bond against buying (or selling) $10 million of notional in the CDS. This type of trade is still quite common due to its simplicity. Unless the cash bond in question is priced at par, however, this approach is not correct, and the analysis will not be accurate. The biggest errors will arise when the bond is trading significantly away from par.

As part of the analysis into the trade, then, we need to assess how much nominal of bond to buy or sell against a set amount of CDS notional, or conversely, how much CDS protection to put on against a set amount of the bond. There is no one way to approach this; the key is the assumption made about the recovery rate in the event of default. In practice, traders will adopt one of the following methods:

❑ *Par/par:* this is a common approach. In such a trade, identical par amounts of the bond and the CDS are traded. The advantage of this method is that the position is straightforward to maintain. The disadvantage is that the trader is not accurately credit-risk hedged if the bond is priced away from par. The CDS pays out par (minus the deliverable asset or cash value on default) on default, but if the bond is priced above par, greater cash value is at risk in a negative basis trade. Therefore, this approach is recommended for bonds priced near to par or for trades with a long-term horizon. It is not recommended for use with bonds at higher risk of default (for instance, sub-investment-grade bonds), as default events expose this trade to potentially the highest loss; it is also more at risk for anything other than small changes in spread.

❑ *Delta-neutral:* this is an approach similar to that used for duration-weighted bond spread trades such as butterfly/barbell trades (see Choudhry [2004b]). It is appropriate when the maturity of the bond does not match precisely the maturity of the CDS.

❑ *DV01:* this approach sets the CDS notional relative to the actual price of the bond. For example, in a negative basis trade, if the bond is trading at EUR120, then we would buy 120% notional of the CDS. This is a logical approach, and recommended if the bond is trading away from par. An assumption of the recovery rate will influence the choice of hedging approach and the notional amount of CDS protection to buy. This is discussed in the next section.

Hedging and Risk

Basis trades are termed as "arbitrage" trades, but strictly speaking are not pure arbitrage trades because they are not risk free. More accurately, they should be called relative value trades. Here, we discuss some issues in unhedged risk.

For instance, the coupon on the bond is not hedged: to do this, we would need to put on a series of coupon strips synthetically to hedge each coupon payable during the life of the bond. In the event of default, the timing of default is crucial; if this occurs just prior to a coupon payment, the actual loss on the trade will be higher than if default occurred just after a coupon payment. In either case, the CDS position does not protect against coupon risk, so remains unhedged.

Another risk factor is the recovery rate assumed for the bond. The rate of recovery cannot be hedged, and the actual recovery after event of default will impact the final profit/loss position. The impact is greatest for bonds that are priced significantly away from par. To illustrate this, consider a bond priced at $110.00. To hedge a long position of $10 million of this bond, assume we buy protection in $11 million nominal of the CDS. We do not use a par/par approach because otherwise we would be underhedged. Now consider, in the event of default, the following recovery rates:

❑ 0% recovery: we receive $11 million on the CDS, and lose $11 million ($1.10 \times 10,000,000$) on the bond, so net we are flat.

❑ 50% recovery: we receive $5.5 million on the CDS, and lose $6 million on the bond (the bond loss is $5 million nominal, and so we receive back $5 million, having paid out $11 million), so net we are down $500,000.

So, in other words, under a 50% recovery rate scenario, we are underhedged still, and would need more notional of CDS to cover the loss on the bond. If the recovery rate is 30%, we will gain on the position, while the higher over 50% it is, we will lose progressively more. Note that the reverse analysis applies when the bond is priced below par. Overall, then, we conclude that the assumption of the recovery rate must influence the notional size of the CDS position.

Generally, the market assumes the following recovery rates:

❑ Investment-grade: 40%
❑ Insurance companies and corporates: 30%
❑ Sub-investment-grade: 20%

Some banks assume a 50% recovery rate in their pricing models. One more robust approach might be to take into account historical data of actual defaults and ultimate recovery rates. At the current time, however, some markets, notably those in Europe and Asia, suffer from a paucity of data. So, for the time being, market participants use assumed recovery rates.

Trade Examples

Here, we illustrate the concept of basis trading with hypothetical trade ideas. For the purposes of this hypothetical illustration, we determine at the outset to run the trade for a 1-month time horizon, so after 1 month, we unwind the trade and see how the trade idea has performed, by checking market prices at the time of the unwind (that is, 1 month later). In reality, we may have a longer horizon, or keep running a trade that is offside because our view is a longer-term one.

Positive Basis Trade

In a positive basis trade, the CDS trades above the cash spread, which can be measured using the ASW spread or the Z-spread.[5]

---

5. See Chapter 2 for a description of the different ways to measure the basis and an example of a Z-spread calculation.

The potential arbitrage trade is to sell the basis—that is, sell the cash bond and sell protection on the same reference name. We would do this if we expect the basis to converge or narrow.

To illustrate this, we describe an example of a basis trade in France Telecom. The cash side of the trade is a euro-denominated bond issued by France Telecom, the 3.625% 2015, rated A3/A–, and which is trading on December 8, 2005, as follows:[6]

Bond	France Telecom 3.625% 2015
ISIN	FR0010245555
Maturity	October 14, 2015
Price	97.52–97.62 clean
ASW	42.9 bps
Z-spread	45.2 bps
CDS price	77–87 bps (10-year CDS)
Repo rate	2.06–2.02 (Libor minus 35 bps)

FIGURE 6.3 *Asset-swap spread on screen ASW, France Telecom 3.625% 2015 bond, December 9, 2005*

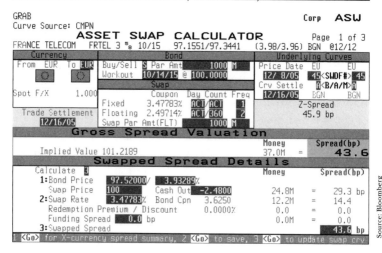

6. Prices are taken from the BLOOMBERG PROFESSIONAL® service (bond and repo) and market makers (CDS).

FIGURE 6.4 *Cash-CDS basis for France Telecom, December 9, 2005*

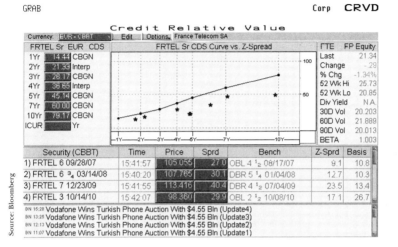

The asset-swap spreads can be seen in **FIGURE 6.3** (they are slightly different from the levels quoted above because the screens were printed the next day and the market had moved). This is Bloomberg screen ASW for the bond. The basis for this bond is positive, as shown in **FIGURE 6.4**, which is Bloomberg screen CRVD.

From the above, we see that the basis is $(77 - 45.2)$, or $+31.8$ basis points. If we have the view that the bond will underperform, or that the basis will otherwise narrow and go toward zero and/or negative, we will sell the basis. We consider historical data on the basis during our analysis, as shown in **FIGURE 6.5**, which is from screen BQ and shows the 1-year historical ASW spread against the 5-year CDS spread.[7]

---

7. Our view on where the basis is going may be based on any combination of factors; these can include speculation about future direction based on historical trade patterns, specific company intelligence such as expectations of a takeover or other buyout, views on credit quality, and so on. We do not discuss the rationale behind the trades in this book, which are the personal view of the individual trader, merely the trade mechanics!

FIGURE 6.5 *1-year historical CDS-ASW spread, France Telecom, December 2005*

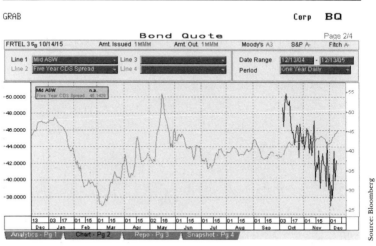

Source: Bloomberg

The trade is put on in the following terms:

❑ Sell EUR 6 million nominal of the bond at 97.52 clean price, 98.1158 dirty price.

❑ Sell protection EUR 5.85 million notional CDS at 77 bps.

Because we are shorting the bond, we fund it in reverse repo, which is done at 2.02%, or Libor minus 35 bps.

The credit risk on the bond position is hedged using the CDS. The interest-rate risk (DV01) is hedged using Bund futures contracts. The hedge calculation is a straightforward one, and uses the ratio of the respective DV01 of the bond and futures contract; see Choudhry (2005) for the hedge calculation mechanics.[8] From this, we determine that we need to buy 52 lots of the Bund future to hedge the bond position.

---

8. The hedge calculation is based on a ratio of basis-point values (DV01) of the bond to be hedged and the futures contract. See Tables 6.3 and 6.4 for the calculation spreadsheet.

TABLE 6.3 *Futures hedge calculation spreadsheet*

A1	B	C	D
2	**Hedging Bonds with Futures**		
3			
4			
5	$Number\ of\ Contracts = \dfrac{Mbond}{Mfut} \times \dfrac{BPVbond}{BPVfut}$		
6			
7			
8			
9			
10	**Inputs**		
11			
12	**Nominal Value of the Bond (Mbond)**	10,000,000.00	
13			
14	**Nominal Value of Futures Contract (Mfut)**	100,000.00	
15			
16	**BPV of the Futures CTD Bond**	7.484	
17			
18	**Conversion Factor of CTD**	0.852	
19			
20	**BPV of the Bond (BPVbond)**	7.558	
21			
22	BPV of the Future (BPVfut)	8.780	
23			
24			
25	**Number of Contracts to Hedge**	**86.083**	
26			
27			
28			

For readers' reference, we show the DV01 hedge calculation in **TABLE 6.3**, which is the Excel spreadsheet used to determine the futures hedge.[9] Note that the example shown is for a hypothetical hedge, not our specific example—we show it here for

---

9. The hedge spreadsheet was written by Stuart Turner and is reproduced with permission.

TABLE 6.4 *Table 6.3 showing Microsoft Excel formulas*

A1	B	C	D
2	**Hedging Bonds with Futures**		
3			
4			
5	$Number\ of\ Contracts = \dfrac{Mbond}{Mfut} \times \dfrac{BPVbond}{BPVfut}$		
6			
7			
8			
9			
10	**Inputs**		
11			
12	**Nominal Value of the Bond (Mbond)**	10,000,000.00	
13			
14	**Nominal Value of Futures Contract (Mfut)**	100,000.00	
15			
16	**BPV of the Futures CTD Bond**	7.484	
17			
18	**Conversion Factor of CTD**	0.852	
19			
20	**BPV of the Bond (BPVbond)**	7.558	
21			
22	BPV of the Future (BPVfut)	=C16/C18	
23			
24			
25	**Number of Contracts to Hedge**	=((C12/C14)*(C20/C22))	
26			
27			
28			

instructional purposes. **TABLE 6.4** shows the Excel formulas.

The analysis is undertaken with reference to Libor, not absolute levels such as the yield-to-maturity. The cash flows are:

Sell bond:	pay 42.9 bps
Sell protection:	receive 62 bps

In addition, the reverse repo position is 35 bps below Libor.

Because it represents interest income, we consider this spread a funding loss, so we incorporate this into the funding calculation; that is, we also pay 35 bps. We ignore the futures position for funding purposes. This is a net carry of

$$62 - (42.9 + 35)$$

or –15.9 basis points. In other words, the net carry for this position is negative. Funding cost must form part of the trade analysis. Funding has a greater impact on the trade net p&l the longer it is kept on. If the trade is maintained over 1 month, the funding impact will not be significant if we generated, say, 5 bps gain in the basis, because that is 5 bps over a 10-year horizon (the maturity of the bond and CDS), the present value of which will exceed the 15.9 bps loss on 1 month's funding. If the position is maintained over a year, the impact of the funding cost will be greater.

Position After 1 Month

On January 10, 2006, we record the following prices for the France Telecom bond and reference name:

Bond	France Telecom 3.625% 2015
Price	98.35–98.45
ASW	42.0 bps
Z-spread	43.8 bps
CDS price	76–80 bps

Spreads are shown in **FIGURE 6.6**.

To unwind this position, we would take the other side of the CDS quote, so the basis is now at (80 − 43.8), or 36.2 basis points. In other words, it has not gone the way we expected, but has widened. Because we sold the basis, the position has lost money if we unwind it now. The decision to unwind would be based on the original trade strategy: if the trader's time

FIGURE 6.6 *France Telecom bond YAS page for asset-swap and Z-spreads, January 10, 2006*

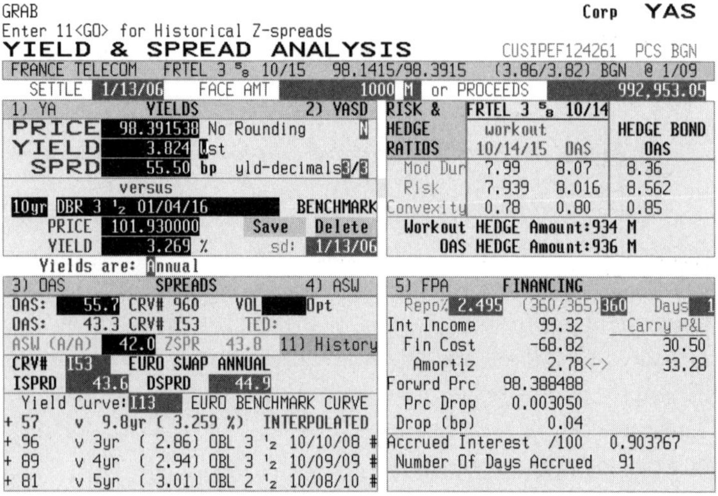

horizon was 6 months or longer, then the decision may be made to continue holding the position. If the trader's time horizon was shorter, it is probably sensible to cut one's losses now. Note that this trade is running at negative net carry, so it incurs a carry loss if maintained, irrespective of where the basis is going.

Negative Basis Trade

In general, it is more common to observe a positive basis than a negative basis, for most market sectors. That said, negative basis observations are not uncommon. In the event of a negative basis condition, the potential arbitrage is to buy the basis—that is, to buy the bond and buy protection on the same reference name. We illustrate such a trade here.

The bond identified here was observed as trading at a negative basis on December 8, 2005. It is the Degussa AG 5.125% of December 2013, which is a euro-denominated bond rated Baa1/BBB+. Its terms are as follows:

FIGURE 6.7 *Degussa 5.125% 2013 bond, asset-swap page, December 9, 2005*

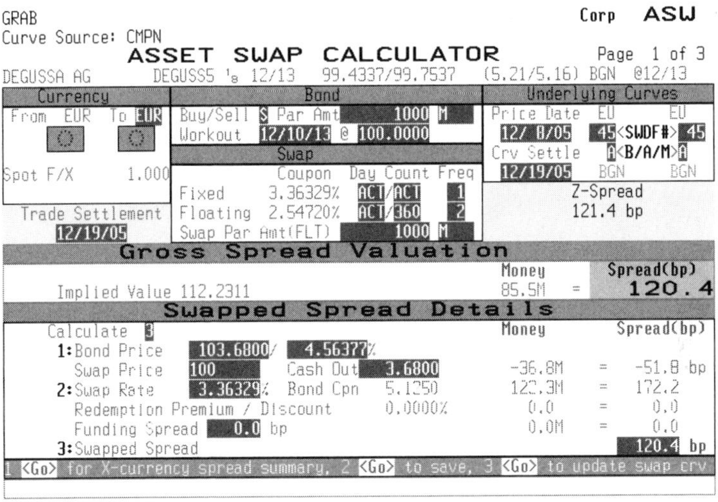

Source: Bloomberg

Bond	Degussa AG 5.125%
	December 2013
ISIN	XS0181557454
Maturity	December 10, 2013
Price	103.68
ASW	121.6
Z-spread	122.7
CDS price	5-year: 75–80
	7-year: 95–105
	10-year: 113–123
	Interpolated 8-year offer: 111 bps
Repo rate	2.44% (Libor + 2)

These rates are seen in **FIGURE 6.7**, the ASW page for this bond, while the basis and basis history are seen in **FIGURES 6.8** and **6.9**, respectively. The basis is (111 − 122.7), or −11.7 basis points. We expect the basis to widen—that is, move from negative

FIGURE 6.8 *Cash-CDS basis, Degussa AG, December 9, 2005*

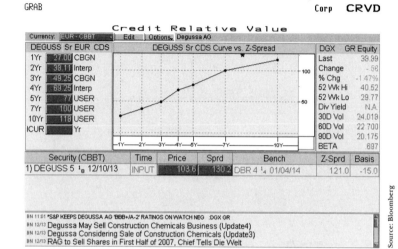

FIGURE 6.9 *1-year CDS-ASW spread, Degussa AG, December 9, 2005*

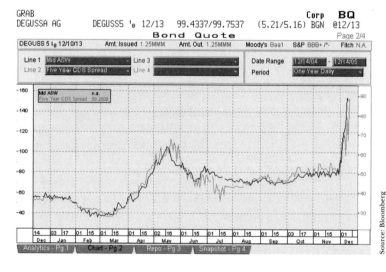

toward zero, and then into positive territory. We therefore buy the bond, and buy protection on the Degussa name. The interest-rate hedge is put on in the same way as before; again, we weight the CDS notional amount to match the risk of the bond because the bond is trading away from par, and so a greater amount of CDS notional is required.

The trade cash flows are as follows:

Buy bond	receive 121.6 bps
Buy protection	pay 111 bps
Repo	pay 2 bps

This is a net carry of +8.6 bps, so this trade runs at a funding gain each day. We expect the basis to widen, at which point we will unwind the trade to extract our profit.

Position After 1 Month

On January 10, 2006, we record the following prices for the Degussa bond and reference name:

Bond	Degussa AG 5.125% December 2013
Price	101.75
ASW	153.2 bps
Z-spread	155.8 bps
CDS price	152–162

Spreads are shown in **FIGURE 6.10**.

The basis is $(152 - 155.8)$, or -3.8 basis points, that is, it has become less negative. The basis has widened, as we expected, and is now in profit. The p&l is positive, and is $(-11.7 - (-3.8))$, or 7.9 basis points, together with the funding gain accrued each day. We can unwind the trade to take profit now—or continue to run it, at a net positive carry, if we expect the basis to move further in the same direction, and then into positive territory.

FIGURE 6.10 *Asset-swap and Z-spreads for Degussa bond, December 10, 2006*

GRAB   Corp **YAS**

YIELD & SPREAD ANALYSIS   CUSIPED23B304   PCS BGN
DEGUSSA AG   DEGUSS5 '8 12/13 101.4342/101.7542 (4.90/4.85) BGN @ 1/09
   SETTLE 1/13/06   FACE AMT   1000 M or PROCEEDS   1,022,273.97

					RISK &	DEGUSS 5 '8 12/1	
1) YA	YIELDS		2) YASD		HEDGE	workout	HEDGE BOND
PRICE	101.750000 No Rounding		N		RATIOS	12/10/13 OAS	OAS
YIELD	4.852 Ust				Mod Dur	6.37 6.45	6.79
SPRD	166.50 bp yld-decimals8/8				Risk	6.512 6.597	7.293
versus					Convexity	0.51 0.52	0.56

8yr DBR 4 '4 01/04/14   BENCHMARK
   PRICE 107.380000   Save Delete   Workout HEDGE Amount:898 M
   YIELD 3.187 %   sd: 1/13/06   OAS HEDGE Amount:905 M
   Yields are: Annual

3) OAS	SPREADS	4) ASW	5) FPA	FINANCING	
OAS: 165.0 CRV# 960	VOL Opt		Repo% 2.495 (360/365)360	Days 1	
OAS: 152.9 CRV# 153	TED:		Int Income 140.41	Carry P&L	
ASW (A/A) 153.2 ZSPR 155.8	11) History		Fin Cost -70.85	69.56	
CRV# 153 EURO SWAP ANNUAL			Amortiz -7.71<->	61.85	
ISPRD 154.8 DSPRD 158.0			Forwrd Prc 101.743044		

   Yield Curve:113 EURO BENCHMARK CURVE   Prc Drop 0.006956
+ 167 v 7.9yr (3.184 %) INTERPOLATED   Drop (bp)   0.09
+ 199 v 3yr (2.87) OBL 3 '2 10/10/08 # Accrued Interest /100 0.477397
+ 191 v 4yr (2.94) OBL 3 '2 10/09/09 # Number Of Days Accrued   34
+ 184 v 5yr (3.01) OBL 2 '2 10/08/10 #

Source: Bloomberg

Notice how the gain itself is small, just a few basis points. Arbitrage basis trading in government bonds is often undertaken in very large size for precisely this reason, because the small potential gain means that to make the trade worthwhile, we have to deal in size. This is not always possible in corporate markets because of smaller issue sizes and lower liquidity levels in the cash market.

EXAMPLE 6.1 *Negative Basis Trade: British Airways PLC*

In this example, we illustrate an unusual example of a reference name trading at large negative basis. The reference name is British Airways PLC, which was experiencing credit downgrade issues during 2005—both general issues relevant to its (airline) sector, and specific issues associated with its passenger performance and industrial relations. An observation of the negative basis spread, which widened considerably in a short time, suggested that the spread would narrow again (heading toward positive territory) over the next 3 to 6 months.

Accordingly, a negative basis trade was considered an appropriate trade. Details of the bond being purchased, the 7.25% of August 2016, are shown in **FIGURE 6.11**. The performance of the basis in the 3 months preceding the trade start date is given in **FIGURE 6.12**, which is screen BQ from the BLOOMBERG PROFESSIONAL® service and shows the CDS-ASW spread during this time. Note how the basis, already negative, moves into greater negative territory quite quickly in early May 2005.

FIGURE 6.11 *Bloomberg page DES for British Airways 7.25% 2016 bond*

DES P174 Corp **DES**

SECURITY DESCRIPTION Page 1/ 2

BRITISH AIRWAYS BAB7 ¼ 08/23/16 108.9200/109.3600 (7.50/7.44) BGN @17:00

ISSUER INFORMATION	IDENTIFIERS	1) Additional Sec Info
Name BRITISH AIRWAYS	Common 013358214	2) Multi Cpn Display
Type Airlines	ISIN XS0133582147	3) ALLQ
Market of Issue Euro Non-Dollar	BB number EC4290101	4) Corporate Actions
SECURITY INFORMATION	RATINGS	5) Par Cds Spreads
Country GB Currency GBP	Moody's Ba2	6) Ratings
Collateral Type Sr Unsub	S&P BB-	7) Custom Notes
Calc Typ(133)MULTI-COUPON	Composite BB-	8) Identifiers
Maturity 8/23/2016 Series		9) Fees/Restrictions
MAKE WHOLE	ISSUE SIZE	10) Additional Note Pg
Coupon 7 ¼ Fixed	Amt Issued/Outstanding	11) Sec. Specific News
S/A **ACT/ACT**	GBP 250,000.00 (M)/	12) Involved Parties
Announcement Dt 7/26/01	GBP 250,000.00 (M)	13) Issuer Information
Int. Accrual Dt 8/23/01	Min Piece/Increment	14) Pricing Sources
1st Settle Date 8/23/01	1,000.00/ 1,000.00	15) Related Securities
1st Coupon Date 2/23/02	Par Amount 1,000.00	16) Issuer Web Page
Iss Pr 99.8730Reoffer 99.873	BOOK RUNNER/EXCHANGE	
SPR @ FPR 215.00 vs UKT 8 12/15	BARCLY,UBS	65) Old DES
NO PROSPECTUS	Multiple	66) Send as Attachment

CPN STEPS UP/DOWN IF RATINGS DOWNGRD/UPGRD BY MOODY'S & S&P; PLEASE SEE ADD NOTE PAGE. CALL @HIGHER OF UKT 8% 12/7/15 OR 100%. PROV CALL/PUT. UNSEC'D.

Source: Bloomberg

FIGURE 6.12 *BA bond CDS-ASW basis performance, March 2005–May 2005*

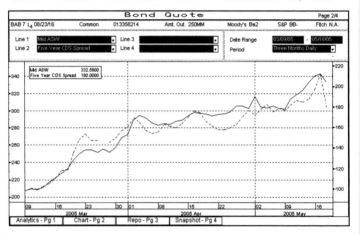

FIGURE 6.13 *BA bond CDS-ASW basis performance, March 2005–October 2005*

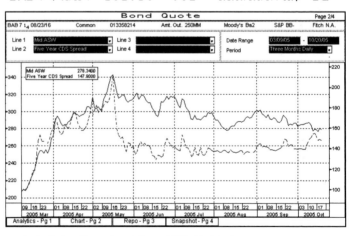

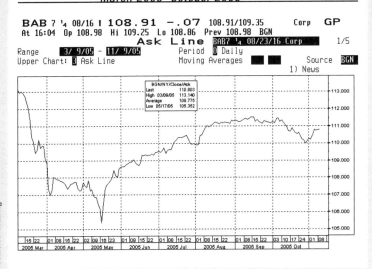

FIGURE 6.14 *BA bond price performance,*
March 2005–October 2005

The trade is put on May 18, 2005, at the following terms:

☐ Buy £5 million BAB 7.25% 2016 bond
☐ Price £106.41 (yield 7.878%)
☐ Buy CDS protection £5 million notional

The CDS spread is 180 basis points (bps). At the ASW spread of 332.58, this represents a basis of −152 bps. On October 17, 2005, we unwind the trade. The price of the bond is now £110.43 (yield is 7.337%), and the CDS spread is 152.6 bps. At an ASW spread of 278.8 bps, this represents a basis of −126 bps. So the profit on this trade is 26 bps.[10]

FIGURE 6.13 shows the basis performance from the trade start date to the trade unwind date. We note how the spread has narrowed—as predicted—during the trade term. **FIGURE 6.14** shows the bond price performance, while **FIGURE 6.15** shows how the

---

10. This is gross profit, before factors such as bid-offer spread and hedge costs are taken into account.

FIGURE 6.15 *BA bond CDS-ASW basis performance, March 2005–March 2006*

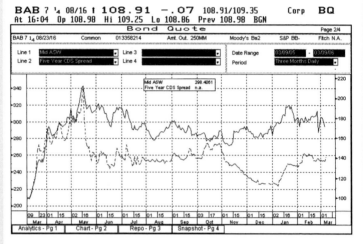

Source: Bloomberg

basis has behaved since the trade was unwound: note how it widened out again in March 2006, the time of writing.

The funding considerations followed those described earlier when we discussed the ThyssenKrupp bond. The bond was funded at Libor-flat, so there is no price impact either way on the funding side. This reflects that all analysis is conducted relative to Libor-flat. Because, in this case, the funding is at L-flat, there is no impact. The interest-rate hedge can be carried out with futures contracts, the benchmark bond (in this case gilts), or with an interest-rate swap. With a swap to matched maturity, we would pay fixed to receive floating, which would be Libor-flat. If we hedge with futures, there

Conclusion

The trades we describe illustrate the mechanics for CDS basis trades, both positive and negative basis. We saw how an arbitrage gain can be made, at theoretically zero credit risk, by

FIGURE 6.16 *Bloomberg screen RRRA, repo funding of BA bond at Libor-flat*

<HELP> for explanation.　　　　　　　　　　　　　　P174 Corp　**RRRA**
Enter <1><GO> to send screen via <MESSAGE> System.
　　　　　REPO/REVERSE REPO ANALYSIS

| BRITISH AIRWAYS BAB7 ¼ 08/23/16 108.9000/109.3400 (7.50/7.45) BGN @15:51 |
| CUSIP:　EC4290101 |

SETTLEMENT DATE	5/23/05	RATE (365)	4.8550%
<SETTLEMENT PRICE>	<MARKET PRICE>	COLLATERAL: 100.0000% OF MONEY
PRICE	106.4100000	106.410000	Y/N, HOLD COLLATERAL PERCENT CONSTANT?	Y
YIELD	7.8778005	7.8778005	Y/N, BUMP ALL DATES FOR WEEKENDS/HOLIDAYS?	Y
ACCRUED	2.1512431	2.1512431	
FOR 89 DAYS.		ROUNDING 1 1 = NOT ROUNDED
TOTAL	108.5612431	108.561243	2 = ROUND TO NEAREST 1/ 8

| FACE AMT M | 10000 | <OR> | SETTLEMENT MONEY | 10856124.31 |
| <OR> To solve for PRICE: Enter NUMBER of BONDS, SETTLEMENT MONEY & COLLATERAL |
| TERMINATION DATE 6/22/05 | <OR> | TERM (IN DAYS) | 30 |
| ACCRUED 2.876981 FOR 119 DAYS. |

　　　　MONEY AT TERMINATION
WIRED AMOUNT	10,856,124.31
REPO INTEREST	43,320.40
TERMINATION MONEY	10,899,444.71
NOTES:

are no funding issues. If we hedge with a gilt, we need to note the reverse repo rate applicable on the gilt, in case it goes special during the term of the trade. If it does not, then the gain on lending funds against gilts will be matched on the other side in what we pay out for shorting the gilt—both rates will be at sub-Libor and should have no impact. In the actual case of this bond, the hedge was undertaken with a matched-maturity interest-rate swap.

Finally, **FIGURE 6.16** shows the Bloomberg screen RRRA, used to calculate cash flows when we fund the BA bond in repo. The trade was funded at 1-month intervals in repo.

buying or selling the basis, provided our initial view is correct. Opportunities for basis trading are rare, and often require good market intelligence on specific corporate names, which can be used to formulate views on these names. Hence, an expertise in credit analysis is essential. In addition, liquidity levels in the cash Eurobond market can be low, depending on the name, and should therefore also be considered when formulating the trade idea.

References

Choudhry, M. 2004a. *Structured credit products: Credit derivatives and synthetic securitisation.* Singapore: John Wiley & Sons.

———. 2004b. *Fixed income markets: Instruments, applications, mathematics.* Singapore: John Wiley & Sons.

———. 2005. *Corporate bond markets: Instruments and applications.* Singapore: John Wiley & Sons.

APPENDIXES

143

APPENDIX I

Description of Bloomberg Screen CDSW

S creen CDSW on the BLOOMBERG PROFESSIONAL® service, an example of which was shown in Figure 1.7, is an implementation of the procedure for pricing a CDS described in Hull and White (2000). The input used in the model to price the CDS contract is one of the three described in Chapter 1. The Bloomberg links the market in CDS prices and the cash bond market with issuer default probabilities.

To calculate the present value of the CDS fee leg (premium leg), the Bloomberg uses the curve of probabilities of default of the reference entity. To calculate the expected present value of the CDS contingent leg, it requires additionally an assumption on the payoff in the case of default; for this, it uses $[(\text{par}-R)+\text{Accrued}]$, where R is the recovery rate. The theoretical value of the CDS is then the difference in the expected present values of the two legs.

Calculating the Default Probability Curve

Given a curve of par CDS spreads (spreads of CDSs of various maturities, each with net present value of zero), the system calculates an implied default probability curve by using a bootstrap procedure. Thus, it finds a default probability curve such that all given CDS contracts have zero value. An alternative procedure is that, given a curve of risky par coupon rates (bond yields), the system

145

FIGURE AI.1 *Transforming curves*

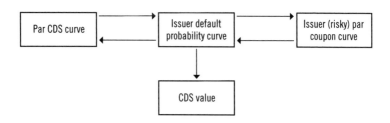

calculates the default probability curve implied by this curve, again using a bootstrap process. The assumption is made that in the case of default of a bond, its value drops to a fraction R of par.

Calculating an Implied Issuer Par Coupon Curve (the "Risky Curve")

If a default probability curve is known, the system can compute a corresponding curve of par coupon rates, corresponding to the size of the coupons an issuer of bonds will have to pay, in order to compensate investors for the default risk they are taking on. In other words, given the par CDS curve, the issuer default probability curve, or the issuer (risky) par coupon curve, the system transforms it into the other two curves (see **FIGURE AI.1**).

Liquidity Premium

The observed spread between an issuer par curve and the risk-free par curve reflects a liquidity premium as well as default risk. The liquidity premium field is a flat spread and selected measure of liquidity. This spread is deducted from the spread between the risky and the risk-free curves before calculation of the default probabilities. A market convention for the liquidity premium is the spread between AAA rates and the interbank swap rate. This spread generally lies within a 0 to 25 basis-point magnitude. The screen defaults to 0 bps.

Issuer Spread-to-Fair Value

The Bloomberg assigns a relevant fair market curve to each bond in accordance with its currency, industry sector, and credit rating (for example, USD A-rated utilities). It also assigns an option-adjusted spread to each issuer, so that the default probability analysis becomes issuer-specific rather than industry-specific.[1]

References

Choudhry, M. 2001. *The bond and money markets: Strategy, trading, analysis.* Oxford: Butterworth-Heinemann.

Hull, J., and A. White. 2000. Valuing credit default swaps I: No counterparty default risk. *Journal of Derivatives* 8 (1) (Fall): 29–40.

1. See Choudhry (2001) for more information on option-adjusted spread.

The Market Approach to CDS Pricing

The market approach to CDS pricing adopts the same no-arbitrage concept as used in interest-rate swap pricing. This states that, at inception,

PV Fixed leg = PV Floating leg.

Therefore, for a CDS, we set

PV Premium leg = PV Contingent leg.

The present value (PV) of the premium leg is straightforward to calculate, especially if there is no credit event during the life of the CDS. The contingent leg, however, is just that—contingent on occurrence of a credit event. Hence, we need to determine the value of the premium leg at the time of the credit event. This requires us to use default probabilities. We can use historical default rates to determine default probabilities, or back them out using market CDS prices. The latter approach is in fact the *implied probabilities* approach.

Default Probabilities

To price a CDS, we need the answers to two basic questions:
- ❑ What is the probability of a credit event?
- ❑ If a credit event occurs, how much is the protection seller likely to pay? This revolves around an assumed *recovery rate*.

We may also need to know:
- ❑ If a credit event occurs, when does this happen?

Let us consider first the probability of default. One way to obtain default probabilities is to observe credit spreads in the corporate bond market. Riskless investments establish a benchmark riskless interest rate, usually the government bond yield. In the corporate bond market (non–zero default probability), lenders and investors expect to receive a higher return from risky investments. The difference between the risky and riskless rates is the *credit spread*. The credit spread will vary according to:
- ❑ Credit quality (for example, credit rating)
- ❑ Maturity
- ❑ Liquidity
- ❑ Supply and demand

Of these factors, one of the most significant is the term to maturity. The *term structure of credit spreads* exhibits a number of features. For instance, lower-quality credits trade at a wider spread than higher-quality credits, and longer-dated obligations normally have higher spreads than shorter-dated ones. For example, for a particular sector, they may look like this:
- ❑ 2-year AA: 20 bps
- ❑ 5-year AA: 30 bps
- ❑ 10-year AA: 37 bps

An exception to this is at the very low end of the credit spectrum; for example, we may observe the following yields for CCC-rated assets:

TABLE AII.1 *Hypothetical corporate bond yields and risk spread*

MATURITY *t*	RISK-FREE YIELD *r*	CORPORATE BOND YIELD *r+y*	RISK SPREAD *y*
0.5	3.57%	3.67%	0.10%
1.0	3.70%	3.82%	0.12%
1.5	3.81%	3.94%	0.13%
2.0	3.95%	4.10%	0.15%
2.5	4.06%	4.22%	0.16%
3.0	4.16%	4.32%	0.16%
3.5	4.24%	4.44%	0.20%
4.0	4.33%	4.53%	0.20%
4.5	4.42%	4.64%	0.22%
5.0	4.45%	4.67%	0.22%

❑ 2-year CCC: 11%
❑ 5-year CCC: 7.75%
❑ 10-year CCC: 7%

In the case of the CCC rating, this reflects the belief that there is a higher probability of default risk right now rather than 5 years from now, because if the company survives the first few years, the risk of default is much lower later on. This gives rise to lower spreads.

Suppose that the corporate bonds of a particular issuer trade at the yields shown in **TABLE AII.1**.

We calculate the continuously compounded rate of return on

TABLE AII.2 *Default probabilities*

MATURITY t	RISK-FREE YIELD r	CORPORATE BOND YIELD $r+y$
0.5	3.57%	3.67%
1.0	3.70%	3.82%
1.5	3.81%	3.94%
2.0	3.95%	4.10%
2.5	4.06%	4.22%
3.0	4.16%	4.32%
3.5	4.24%	4.44%
4.0	4.33%	4.53%
4.5	4.42%	4.64%
5.0	4.45%	4.67%

the risk-free asset to be

$$e^{rt}.$$

The rate of return on the risky asset is therefore given by

$$e^{(r+y)t}.$$

We now calculate the default probability assuming zero recovery of the asset value following default. On this assumption, if the probability of default is p, then an investor should be indifferent between an expected return of

$$(1-p)e^{(r+y)t}$$

RISK SPREAD y	CUMULATIVE PROBABILITY OF DEFAULT	ANNUAL PROBABILITY OF DEFAULT
0.10%	0.050%	0.050%
0.12%	0.120%	0.070%
0.13%	0.195%	0.075%
0.15%	0.299%	0.104%
0.16%	0.399%	0.100%
0.16%	0.479%	0.080%
0.20%	0.698%	0.219%
0.20%	0.797%	0.099%
0.22%	0.985%	0.188%
0.22%	1.094%	0.109%

on the risky corporate bond, and

$$e^{rt}.$$

Setting these two expressions equal, we have

$$(1 - p)e^{(r+y)t} = e^{rt}. \qquad (AII.1)$$

Solving for p gives

$$p = 1 - e^{-yt}. \qquad (AII.2)$$

Using $p = 1 - e^{-yt}$, we can calculate therefore the probabilities of default from credit spreads that were shown in Table AII.1. These are shown in **TABLE AII.2**.

TABLE AII.3 _Cumulative default probabilities_

MATURITY t	RISK-FREE YIELD r	CORPORATE BOND YIELD $r+y$	RISK SPREAD y	CUMULATIVE PROBABILITY OF DEFAULT
0.5	3.57%	3.67%	0.10%	0.071%
1.0	3.70%	3.82%	0.12%	0.171%
1.5	3.81%	3.94%	0.13%	0.279%
2.0	3.95%	4.10%	0.15%	0.427%
2.5	4.06%	4.22%	0.16%	0.570%
3.0	4.16%	4.32%	0.16%	0.684%
3.5	4.24%	4.44%	0.20%	0.997%
4.0	4.33%	4.53%	0.20%	1.139%
4.5	4.42%	4.64%	0.22%	1.407%
5.0	4.45%	4.67%	0.22%	1.563%

For example,

$$p_{0,5} = 1 - e^{-0.0025 \times 5} = 1.094\%$$

is the cumulative probability of default over the complete 5-year period, while

$$p_{4,5} = p_{0,5} - p_{0,4} = 0.109\%$$

is the probability of default in year 5.

We then extend the analysis to an assumption of a specified recovery rate following default. If the probability of default is p, and the recovery rate is R, then an investor should now be indifferent between an expected return of

$$(1 - p)e^{(r+y)t} + Rpe^{(r+y)t} \qquad \text{(AII.3)}$$

on the risky corporate bond, and e^{rt} on the (risk-free) government bond.

Again, setting these two expressions equal, and solving for p gives[1]

$$(1 - p)e^{(r+y)t} + Rpe^{(r+y)t} = e^{rt}$$

$$p = \frac{1 - e^{-yt}}{1 - R} \; . \qquad \text{(AII.4)}$$

Using this formula and assuming a recovery rate of 30%, we calculate the cumulative default probabilities shown in **TABLE AII.3**.

---

1. The steps in between are:

$$(1 - p)e^{(r+y)t} = e^{rt}$$
$$(1 - p)e^{rt}.e^{yt} = e^{rt}$$
$$(1 - p)e^{-yt} = 1$$
$$1 - p = e^{-yt}$$
$$p = 1 - e^{-yt}$$

Incorporating the recovery rate R, we have the following steps:

$$1 - p + pR = e^{-yt}$$
$$-p + pR = e^{-yt} - 1$$
$$-p(1 - R) = e^{-yt} - 1$$
$$-p = \frac{e^{-yt} - 1}{1 - R}$$
$$p = \frac{1 - e^{-yt}}{1 - R}$$

FIGURE AII.1 *Binary process of survival or default*

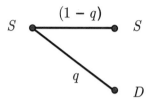

FIGURE AII.2 *Binary process of survival or default over multiple periods*

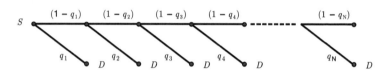

For example,

$$p_{0,5} = \frac{1 - e^{-0.0022 \times 5}}{1 - 0.30} = 1.563\%$$

is the cumulative probability of default over the 5-year period.

We now expand the analysis to default and survival probabilities. Consider what happens to a risky asset over a specific period of time. There are just two possibilities, which are:

❑ There is a credit event, and the asset defaults.
❑ There is no credit event, and the asset survives.

Let us call these outcomes D (for default), having a probability q, and S (for survival), having a probability of $(1 - q)$. We can represent this as a binary process, shown in **FIGURE AII.1**.

Over multiple periods, this binary process can be illustrated as shown in **FIGURE AII.2**.

As shown in Figure AII.2, the probability of survival to period N is then

$$PSN = (1 - q1) \times (1 - q2) \times (1 - q3)$$
$$\times (1 - q4) \times \ldots \times (1 - qN), \qquad (AII.5)$$

while the probability of default in any period N is

$$PSN\text{-}1 \times qN = PSN\text{-}1 - PSN. \qquad (AII.6)$$

Given these formulas, we can now price a CDS contract.

Pricing a CDS Contract

Given a set of default probabilities, we can calculate the fair premium for a CDS, which is the market approach first described in Chapter 1. To do this, consider a CDS as a series of contingent cash flows, the cash flows depending upon whether a credit event occurs. This is shown in **FIGURE AII.3**. The symbols are

s = the CDS premium
k = the day count fraction when default occurred
R = the recovery rate

We wish first to value the premium stream given no default, shown in Figure AII.3(a). The expected PV of the stream of CDS premiums over time can be calculated as

$$PVS_{nd} = s \sum_{j=1}^{N} DF_j PS_j T_{j-1,j}, \qquad (AII.7)$$

where

PVS_{nd} = the expected present value of the stream of CDS premiums if there is no default
s = the CDS spread (fee or premium)
DF_j = the discount factor for period j
PS_j = the probability of survival through period j
$T_{j-1,j}$ = the length of time of period j (expressed as a fraction of a year).

FIGURE AII.3 *CDS contingent cash flows*

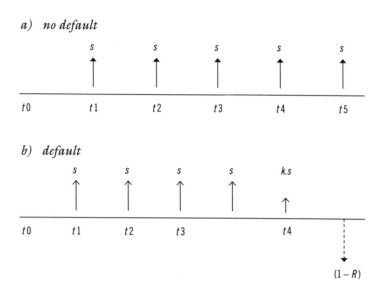

a) *no default*

b) *default*

We now require an expression for the value of the premium stream given default, which are the cash flows shown in Figure AII.3(b). If a default occurs exactly halfway through period C, and the CDS makes the default payment at the end of that period, the expected present value of the fees received is

$$PVS_d = s \sum_{j=1}^{C} DF_j PS_j T_{j-1,j} + s.DF_C PD_C \frac{T_{C-1,C}}{2}, \quad \text{(AII.8)}$$

while the value of the default payment is

$$(1-R) DF_C PD_C, \quad \text{(AII.9)}$$

where

PVS_d = the expected present value of the stream of CDS premiums if there is default in period C

PD_C = the probability of default in period C

R = the recovery rate,

and the other terms are as before.

On the no-arbitrage principle, which is the same approach used to price interest-rate swaps, for a CDS to be fairly priced, the expected value of the premium stream must equal the expected value of the default payment.

Because default can occur in any period j, we can therefore write

$$s\sum_{j=1}^{N} DF_j PS_j T_{j-1,j} + s\sum_{j=1}^{N} DF_j PD_j \frac{T_{j-1,j}}{2} = (1-R)\sum_{j=1}^{N} DF_j PD_j .$$

(AII.10)

In equation (AII.10) the first part of the left-hand side (LHS) is the expected present value of the stream of premium payments if no default occurs, and the second part of the LHS is the expected present value of the accrued premium payment in the period when default occurs. The right-hand side (RHS) of equation (AII.10) is the expected present value of the default payment in the period when default occurs.

Rearranging this expression gives the fair premium s for the CDS, shown as equation (AII.11).

$$s = \frac{(1-R)\sum_{j=1}^{N} DF_j PD_j}{\sum_{j=1}^{N} DF_j PS_j T_{j-1,j} + \sum_{j=1}^{N} DF_j PD_j \frac{T_{j-1,j}}{2}}$$

(AII.11)

TABLE AII.4 *Calculation of CDS prices*

Cell	B	C	D	E
3				
4				
5	MATURITY t	SPOT RATES	DISCOUNT FACTORS DF_j	SURVIVAL PROBABILITY PS_j
6	0.5	3.57%	0.9826	0.9993
7	1.0	3.70%	0.9643	0.9983
8	1.5	3.81%	0.9455	0.9972
9	2.0	3.95%	0.9254	0.9957
10	2.5	4.06%	0.9053	0.9943
11	3.0	4.16%	0.8849	0.9932
12	3.5	4.24%	0.8647	0.9900
13	4.0	4.33%	0.8440	0.9886
14	4.5	4.42%	0.8231	0.9859
15	5.0	4.45%	0.8044	0.9844
16				
17	RECOVERY RATE			
18	0.3			

Example Calculation

We have shown, then, that the price of a CDS contract can be calculated from the spot rates and default probability values given earlier. In this example, we assume that the credit event (default)

F	G	H	I	J
DEFAULT PROBABILITY PD_j	PROBABILITY-WEIGHTED PVs			
	PV OF RECEIPTS IF NO DEFAULT	PV OF RECEIPTS IF DEFAULT	DEFAULT PAYMENT IF DEFAULT	CDS PREMIUM s
0.0007	0.4910	0.0002	0.0005	0.10%
0.0017	0.9723	0.0006	0.0016	0.17%
0.0028	1.4437	0.0012	0.0035	0.24%
0.0043	1.9044	0.0022	0.0063	0.33%
0.0057	2.3545	0.0035	0.0099	0.42%
0.0068	2.7939	0.0050	0.0141	0.50%
0.0100	3.2220	0.0072	0.0201	0.62%
0.0114	3.6392	0.0096	0.0269	0.74%
0.0141	4.0450	0.0125	0.0350	0.86%
0.0156	4.4409	0.0156	0.0438	0.98%

occurs halfway through the premium period, thus enabling us to illustrate the calculation of the present value of the receipt in the event of default (the second part of the left-hand side of the original no-arbitrage equation [AII.10], the accrual factor) in more straightforward fashion.

TABLE AII.5 *CDS price calculation: Excel spreadsheet formulas*

Cell	B	C	D	E	F	G
3						
4						
5	MATURITY t	SPOT RATES	DISCOUNT FACTORS DF$_j$	SURVIVAL PROBABILITY PS$_j$	DEFAULT PROBABILITY PD$_j$	PV OF RECEIPTS IF IF NO DEFAULT
6	0.5	3.57%	=1/(1+C6)^0.5	=1-F6	0.0007	=SUMPRODUCT($D$6:D6,$E$6:E6)*0.5
7	1.0	3.70%	=1/(1+C7)^1	=1-F7	0.0017	=SUMPRODUCT($D$6:D7,$E$6:E7)*0.5
8	1.5	3.81%	=1/(1+C8)^1.5	=1-F8	0.0028	=SUMPRODUCT($D$6:D8,$E$6:E8)*0.5
9	2.0	3.95%	=1/(1+C9)^2	=1-F9	0.0043	=SUMPRODUCT($D$6:D9,$E$6:E9)*0.5
10	2.5	4.06%	=1/(1+C10)^2.5	=1-F10	0.0057	=SUMPRODUCT($D$6:D10,$E$6:E10)*0.5
11	3.0	4.16%	=1/(1+C11)^3	=1-F11	0.0068	=SUMPRODUCT($D$6:D11,$E$6:E11)*0.5
12	3.5	4.24%	=1/(1+C12)^3.5	=1-F12	0.0100	=SUMPRODUCT($D$6:D12,$E$6:E12)*0.5
13	4.0	4.33%	=1/(1+C13)^4	=1-F13	0.0114	=SUMPRODUCT($D$6:D13,$E$6:E13)*0.5
14	4.5	4.42%	=1/(1+C14)^4.5	=1-F14	0.0141	=SUMPRODUCT($D$6:D14,$E$6:E14)*0.5
15	5.0	4.45%	=1/(1+C15)^5	=1-F15	0.0156	=SUMPRODUCT($D$6:D15,$E$6:E15)*0.5
16						
17	RECOVERY RATE					
18	0.3					

TABLE AII.4 on pages 160 and 161 illustrates the pricing of a CDS contract written on the reference entity whose credit spread premium over the risk-free rate was introduced earlier. The default probabilities were calculated as shown in Table AII.3.

TABLE AII.5 shows the Microsoft Excel formulas used in the calculation spreadsheet.

H	I	J

— PROBABILITY-WEIGHTED PVS ———————————————

PV OF RECEIPTS IF DEFAULT	DEFAULT PAYMENT IF DEFAULT	CDS PREMIUM s
=SUMPRODUCT($D$6:D6,$F$6:F6)*0.5/2	=(1-$B$18)*SUMPRODUCT($D$6:D6,$F$6:F6)	=I6/(G6+H6)
=SUMPRODUCT($D$6:D7,$F$6:F7)*0.5/2	=(1-$B$18)*SUMPRODUCT($D$6:D7,$F$6:F7)	=I7/(G7+H7)
=SUMPRODUCT($D$6:D8,$F$6:F8)*0.5/2	=(1-$B$18)*SUMPRODUCT($D$6:D8,$F$6:F8)	=I8/(G8+H8)
=SUMPRODUCT($D$6:D9,$F$6:F9)*0.5/2	=(1-$B$18)*SUMPRODUCT($D$6:D9,$F$6:F9)	=I9/(G9+H9)
=SUMPRODUCT($D$6:D10,$F$6:F10)*0.5/2	=(1-$B$18)*SUMPRODUCT($D$6:D10,$F$6:F10)	=I10/(G10+H10)
=SUMPRODUCT($D$6:D11,$F$6:F11)*0.5/2	=(1-$B$18)*SUMPRODUCT($D$6:D11,$F$6:F11)	=I11/(G11+H11)
=SUMPRODUCT($D$6:D12,$F$6:F12)*0.5/2	=(1-$B$18)*SUMPRODUCT($D$6:D12,$F$6:F12)	=I12/(G12+H12)
=SUMPRODUCT($D$6:D13,$F$6:F13)*0.5/2	=(1-$B$18)*SUMPRODUCT($D$6:D13,$F$6:F13)	=I13/(G13+H13)
=SUMPRODUCT($D$6:D14,$F$6:F14)*0.5/2	=(1-$B$18)*SUMPRODUCT($D$6:D14,$F$6:F14)	=I14/(G14+H14)
=SUMPRODUCT($D$6:D15,$F$6:F15)*0.5/2	=(1-$B$18)*SUMPRODUCT($D$6:D15,$F$6:F15)	=I15/(G15+H15)

Consider the 1-year CDS premium. From Table AII.4, the 1-year CDS premium is 0.17%. To check this calculation, we observe the expected present value of the premium for the 6-month and 1-year dates, which is

❑ Survival probability × Discount factor × Premium × Day count fraction.

FIGURE AII.4 *Term structure of credit rates*

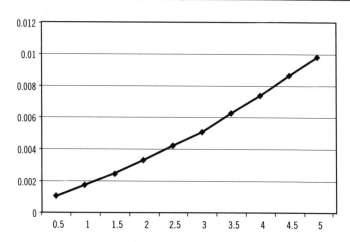

For the 6-month period, this is $0.9993 \times 0.9826 \times 0.0017 \times 0.5$, or 0.0008346.

For the 1-year period, this is $0.9983 \times 0.9643 \times 0.1017 \times 0.5$, or 0.00081826.

The expected present value of the accrued premium if default occurs halfway through a period is

❏ Default probability × Discount factor × Premium × Day count fraction.

For the 6-month period, this is $0.0007 \times 0.9826 \times 0.0017 \times 0.25$, which actually comes out to a negligible value. For the 1-year period, the amount is

$0.0017 \times 0.9643 \times 0.0017 \times 0.25$, which is also negligible.

The total expected value of premium income is 0.00166.

The expected present value of the default payment if payment is made at the end of the period is

❏ Default probability × Discount factor × (1 − Recovery rate), which for the two periods is

FIGURE AII.5 *Term structure of default probabilities*

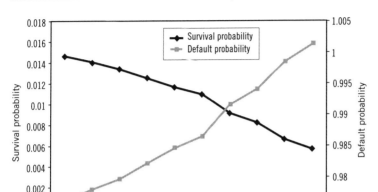

- ❏ 6-month: $0.0007 \times 0.9826 \times (1 - 30\%) = 0.000482$
- ❏ 12-month: $0.0017 \times 0.9643 \times (1 - 30\%) = 0.001148$

So the total expected value of the default payment is 0.00166, which is equal to the earlier calculation. Our present values for both fixed leg and contingent leg are identical, which means we have the correct no-arbitrage value for the CDS contract.

From the CDS premium values, we can construct a term structure of credit rates for this particular reference credit (or reference sector), which is shown in **FIGURE AII.4**. We can also construct a term structure of default probabilities, and this is shown in **FIGURE AII.5**.

Market-Implied Timing of Default from CDS Prices

T he premium payable on a credit default swap (CDS) contract is an explicit valuation of default risk.[1] Given that
the CDS has a specified fixed term to maturity, it is possible by applying break-even analysis to extract a market-implied
timing of default for the reference credit in question. This is
done by calculating the amount of time that has to elapse before
the premium income on the CDS equals the recovery value. By
definition therefore, we require an assumed recovery rate to perform this calculation.

When a credit reference shows signs of distress, the CDS market begins to reflect this by marking the price of a CDS written
on that name higher. This implies the timing of the default event.
For instance, assume that recent market sentiment concerning
ABC PLC suggests that it is about to be downgraded to sub-
investment-grade status, and that default is now a high possibility.
As a result, 5-year quarterly-in-arrears CDS for ABC PLC rises in
price and is now quoted at 2,300 basis points (bps). The recovery

---

1. More accurately, credit event risk, because certain situations short of full default
also constitute a "credit event" under which the CDS contract is terminated and a
payout made by the protection seller.

FIGURE AIII.1 *Default timing calculation, 5-year CDS*

A1	B	C	D
2		Principal	£20,000,000
3		Recovery rate	30%
4			
5	Maturity	5 Year	
6		1 Year	
7	Payment frequency	0.25 Year	
8			
9		Recovery	
10			
11		Without discounting	
12		5.217391304	periods
13		1.304347826	**Years breakeven**
14			
15	To obtain the implied price of default:		
16	Set G9 = 0 by changing C11.		
17	Use "Goal Seek" function.		

rate is expected to be 30% of the company value in the event of default occurring. Given this information, it is possible to get an approximate idea of when the market anticipates a default.

The calculation is shown in **FIGURE AIII.1**, an Excel spreadsheet used to obtain the break-even point value.[2] Cell H10 establishes the difference between the recovery amount and the time-weighted premium income. In this case, the time weighting is quarterly, which is common for most CDS contracts. Initially,

---

2. The spreadsheet was written by Brian Eales and is reproduced with kind permission.

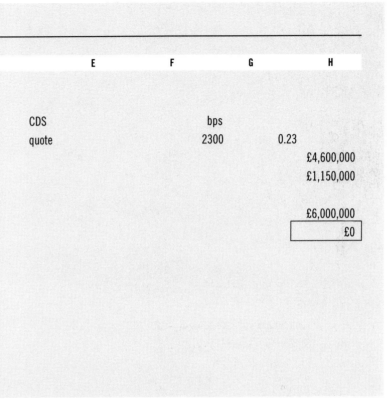

	E	F	G	H
CDS		bps		
quote		2300	0.23	
				£4,600,000
				£1,150,000
				£6,000,000
				£0

this value will not be equal to zero. To establish the (undiscount-ed) break-even point, we apply the "Goal Seek" function. We set the difference in H10 to zero by changing the value in cell D12. Cell D13 converts the number of periods back into years.

In our example, we have a 5-year CDS of £20 million trading at 2,300 basis points spread. £4.6 million would be paid each year for default protection. Assuming a 30% recovery rate, the recovery in the event of default is expected to be £6 million. Ignoring the necessary discounting process, the £6 million will be received as premium in approximately 1.3 years. If this calculation is correct, then selling protection via the CDS will bring in premium income until the default

FIGURE AIII.2 _Excel spreadsheet formulas used in Figure AIII.1_

A1	B	C	D
2		Principal	£20,000,000
3		Recovery rate	30%
4			
5		Maturity	5 Year
6			1 Year
7	Payment frequency		0.25 Year
8			
9			Recovery
10			
11			Without discounting
12			5.217391304 periods
13			=C7*D12 Years breakeven
14			
15	To obtain the implied price of default:		
16	Set G9 = 0 by changing C11.		
17	Use "Goal Seek" function.		

occurs. **FIGURE AIII.2** shows the Excel formulas used in Figure AIII.1.

This type of trading has occurred in a number of lower-rated market sectors. Default timing risk can be seen as a means of achieving diversification of premium income within a portfolio.

	E	F	G	H
CDS		bps		
quote		2300	=F5/10000	
				=D2*G5
				=H6*C7
				£6,000,000
				=H9–H7*D12

GLOSSARY

ABS: See **asset-backed securities**.

ALM: See **asset and liability management**.

amortizing: An amortizing principal is one that decreases during the life of a deal or is repaid in stages during a loan. Amortizing an amount over a period of time also means accruing for it pro rata over the period.

arbitrage: The process of buying securities in one country, currency, or market, and selling identical securities in another to take advantage of price differences. When this is carried out simultaneously, it is, in theory, a risk-free transaction. There are many forms of arbitrage transactions. For instance, in the cash market, a bank might issue a money market instrument in one money center and invest the same amount in another center at a higher rate—such as an issue of 3-month U.S. dollar CDs in the United States at 5.5% and a purchase of 3-month Eurodollar CDs at 5.6%. In the futures market, arbitrage might involve buying 3-month contracts and selling forward 6-month contracts.

arbitrage CDO: A collateralized debt obligation (CDO) that has been issued by an asset manager and in which the collateral is purchased solely for the purpose of securitizing it to exploit the difference in yields ("arbitrage") between the underlying market and securitization market.

asset and liability management (ALM): The practice of matching the term structure and cash flows of an organization's asset and liability portfolios to maximize returns and minimize risk.

asset-backed securities (ABS): Securities that have been issued by a special purpose legal vehicle (SPV) and that are backed by principal and interest payments on existing assets, which have been sold to the SPV by the deal originator. These assets can include commercial bank loans, credit card loans, auto loans, equipment lease receivables, and so on.

asset swap: An interest-rate swap or currency swap used in conjunction with an underlying asset such as a bond investment.

average life: The weighted-average life (WAL) of a bond, the estimated time to return principal based on an assumed prepayment speed. It is the average number of years that each unit of unpaid principal remains outstanding.

balance sheet CDO: A CDO backed by a static pool of assets that were previously on the balance sheet of the originator.

basis: The underlying cash market price minus the futures price. In the case of a bond futures contract, the futures price must be multiplied by the conversion factor for the cash bond in question.

basis point: In interest-rate quotations, 0.01%.

basis smile: The term for a graphic illustration of the basis across credit ratings. Ratings are plotted on the x-axis.

basis swap: An interest-rate swap where both legs are based on floating-rate payments.

bullet: A loan/deposit has a bullet maturity if the principal is all repaid at maturity. See **amortizing**.

calculation agent: An independent third party that is retained to calculate recovery values and other valuations relevant in a terminated credit derivative contract.

call option: An option contract that provides the buyer with the right, but not the obligation, to purchase an amount of the underlying asset at a specified time and prespecified price (the "strike" or exercise price).

cash settlement: In credit derivative markets, the process of settling a terminated contract by means of a cash payment reflecting recovery value of the defaulted asset. Also, a general term indicating settlement the following day.

CDO: See **collateralized debt obligation**.

cheapest-to-deliver: For credit derivatives, the delivery option afforded to the protection buyer in a credit derivative contract on occurrence of a credit event. Subject to certain restrictions on long-dated securities and convertible bonds, the buyer of protection may deliver any equivalent-seniority liability of the reference entity as settlement of the (physically settled) CDS contract.

collateralized debt obligation (CDO): A securitized product that consists of assets, which are bonds, loans, or other assets, that are funded by issuing liabilities in the capital market. The assets may be actively managed by a fund manager. Synthetic CDOs reference assets without actually securitizing them.

contracts for differences: Derivative contracts whose payout is linked to the market value of an underlying asset or index and the difference with a contracted strike value.

cost of carry: The net running cost of holding a position (which may be negative), for example, the cost of borrowing cash to buy a bond less the coupon earned on the bond while holding it.

coupon: The interest payment(s) made by the issuer of a security to the holders, based on the coupon rate and the face value.

cover: To cover an exposure is to deal in such a way as to remove the risk—either by reversing the position, or hedging it by dealing in an instrument with a similar but opposite risk profile. Also, the amount by how much a bond auction is subscribed.

credit default swap (credit swap, default swap): Agreement between two counterparties to exchange disparate cash flows, at least one of which must be tied to the performance of a credit-sensitive asset or to a portfolio or index of such assets. The other cash flow is usually tied to a floating-rate index (such as Libor) or a fixed rate, or is linked to another credit-sensitive asset.

credit derivatives: Financial contracts that involve a potential exchange of payments in which at least one of the cash flows is linked to the performance of a specified underlying credit-sensitive asset or liability.

credit enhancement: A level of investor protection built into a structured finance deal to absorb losses among the underlying assets. This may take the form of cash, "equity" subordinated note tranches, subordinated tranches, cash reserves, excess spread reserve, insurance protection ("wrap"), and so on.

credit loss: See **expected loss**.

credit (or default) risk: The risk that a loss will be incurred if a counterparty to a derivatives transaction does not fulfil its financial obligations in a timely manner.

credit-risk (or default-risk) exposure: The value of the contract exposed to default. If all transactions are marked-to-market each day, such positive market value is the amount of previously recorded profit that might have to be reversed and recorded as a loss in the event of counterparty default.

credit spread: The interest-rate spread between two debt issues of similar duration and maturity, reflecting the relative creditworthiness of the issuers.

credit swap: See **credit default swap**.

currency swap: An agreement to exchange a series of cash flows determined in one currency, possibly with reference to a particular fixed or floating interest payment schedule, for a series of cash flows based in a different currency. See **interest-rate swap**.

default correlation: The degree of covariance between the probabilities of default of a given set of counterparties. For example, in a set of counterparties with positive default correlation, a default by one counterparty suggests an increased probability of a default by another counterparty.

default-risk exposure: See **credit-risk exposure**.

default swap: See **credit default swap**.

deliverable: One of the bonds that is eligible to be delivered by the seller of a bond futures contract at the contract's maturity, according to the specifications of that particular contract. Also used to apply to the deliverable in a terminated CDS contract that is physically settled.

digital credit derivative: A (binary) credit default swap; the contingent payment if default occurs equals a prespecified notional amount, irrespective of the recovery value.

diversity score: A Moody's CDO calculation that assigns to an asset portfolio a numeric value that represents the number of uncorrelated assets theoretically in the portfolio. A low diversity score indicates industry and/or geographic concentration and will be penalized in the ratings process.

DV01: Literally, "Dollar Value of a 01," that is, the change in dollar value for a 1-basis-point change in yield. This is a risk sensitivity measure that shows the level of risk exposure of a bond position, because it estimates the change in bond price for a 1-basis-point parallel shift in the yield curve. Also referred to as PV01 and PVBP. In the CDS market, it refers to the change in present value of a CDS contract for a 1-basis-point change in the contract premium. To avoid confusion with bond market terminology, this is often called *CS*01 in the CDS market.

entity: A legally incorporated company.

equity-linked swap: Swap where one of the cash flows is based on an equity instrument or index, when it is known as an equity index swap.

equivalent life: The weighted average life of the principal of a bond where there are partial redemptions, using the **present values** of the partial redemptions as the weights. See **redeem**.

excess spread: Total cash left over in a securitization, after paying all costs.

expected default rate: Estimate of the most likely rate of default of a counterparty, expressed as a level of probability.

expected (credit) loss: Estimate of the amount a derivatives counterparty is likely to lose as a result of default from a derivatives contract, with a given level of probability. The expected loss of any derivative position can be derived by combining the distributions of credit exposures, rate of recovery, and probabilities of default.

expected rate of recovery: See **rate of recovery**.

face value (nominal amount): The principal amount of a security, generally repaid ("redeemed") all at maturity, but sometimes repaid in stages, on which the **coupon** amounts are calculated.

fixed amount: A prespecified cash payment.

floating rate: An interest rate set with reference to an external index. Also, an instrument paying a floating rate is one where the rate of interest is refixed in line with market conditions at regular intervals, such as every 3 or 6 months. In the current market, an exchange rate determined by market forces with no government intervention.

floating-rate note: Capital market instrument on which the rate of interest payable is refixed in line with market conditions at regular intervals (usually 6 months).

forward: A tailor-made derivative contract that references an underlying asset forward delivery.

forward swap: An interest-rate swap with a forward starting date.

funded: Paid for at trade inception. A funded credit derivative requires full payment of notional value at time of trade.

funding risk: The risk that the funding rate for a borrower rises at the time the loan is renewed.

future: A futures contract is a contract to buy or sell securities or other goods at a future date at a predetermined price. Futures contracts are usually standardized and traded on an exchange.

general collateral (GC): Securities that are not "special," used as collateral against cash borrowing. A repo buyer will accept GC at any time that a specific stock is not quoted as required in the transaction. In the gilts market, GC includes DBVs.

guaranteed investment contract (GIC): A bank account that pays either a fixed rate for its life, or a fixed spread under Libor for its life.

hedging: Protecting against the risks arising from potential market movements in exchange rates, interest rates, or other variables. See **cover**; **arbitrage**; **speculation**.

historic volatility: The actual **volatility** recorded in market prices over a particular period.

implied probabilities: Probabilities that are implied by other market rates or factors and calculated from these factors.

implied volatility: The volatility used by a dealer to calculate an option price; conversely, the volatility implied by the price actually quoted.

interbank: The market in unsecured lending and trading between banks of roughly similar credit quality.

interest-rate swap: An agreement to exchange a series of cash flows determined in one currency, based on fixed or **floating** interest payments on an agreed **notional** principal, for a series of cash flows based in the same currency but on a different interest rate. May be combined with a **currency swap**.

internal rate of return: The yield necessary to discount a series of cash flows to a net present value of zero.

I-spread: The spread in basis points between the yield on a corporate bond and the interest-rate swap curve.

liability swap: An interest-rate swap or currency swap used in conjunction with an underlying liability such as a borrowing. See **asset swap.**

Libid: The London interbank bid rate, the rate at which banks will pay for funds in the interbank market.

Libor (or LIBOR): The London interbank offered rate, the lending rate for all major currencies up to 1 year, set at 11 a.m. each day by the British Bankers' Association (BBA). It is calculated as the average of the quotes set by member banks of the BBA. **FIGURE G.1** on the following page shows the Bloomberg page BBAM1, the daily fix screen for Libor rates, as of March 13, 2006.

liquidity: A word describing the ease with which one can undertake transactions in a particular market or instrument. A market where there are always ready buyers and sellers willing to transact at competitive prices is regarded as liquid. In banking, the term is also used to describe the requirement that a portion of a bank's assets be held in short-term, risk-free instruments—such as government bonds, T-bills, and high-quality certificates of deposit.

long: A long position is a surplus of purchases over sales of a given currency or asset, or a situation that naturally gives rise

FIGURE G.1 *Bloomberg page BBAM1, showing Libor fixes for major currencies, as of March 13, 2006*

BRITISH BANKERS'
ASSOCIATION   Page 1 of 4

03/13   14:51 GMT   [REUTERS] [BBA LIBOR RATES]   Telerate Successor Page 3750
[13/03/06]   RATES AT 11:00 LONDON TIME 13/03/2006   13/03 11:35 GMT

CCY	USD	GBP	CAD	EUR	JPY	EUR 365
O/N	4.54813	4.80875	3.81333	2.59500	SNO.05563	2.63104
1WK	4.56750	4.60750	3.80500	2.60425	0.05563	2.64042
2WK	4.62750	4.57188	3.80333	2.61063	0.05813	2.64689
1MO	4.74875	4.57688	3.81500	2.63288	0.07313	2.66945
2MO	4.81938	4.58000	3.84500	2.65500	0.08750	2.69188
3MO	4.91000	4.58375	3.88500	2.70050	0.10313	2.73801
4MO	4.96225	4.59563	3.92333	2.75338	0.11375	2.79162
5MO	5.02000	4.60875	3.96167	2.80388	0.12500	2.84282
6MO	5.07000	4.62938	4.00000	2.84700	0.13813	2.88654
7MO	5.10875	4.64875	4.03000	2.89263	0.15750	2.93281
8MO	5.14188	4.66750	4.06000	2.93525	0.17625	2.97602
9MO	5.17100	4.68688	4.08667	2.98000	0.20063	3.02139
10MO	5.19538	4.70875	4.11000	3.01975	0.22313	3.06169
11MO	5.21413	4.72813	4.13333	3.05800	0.24250	3.10047
12MO	5.23475	4.74438	4.15333	3.08563	0.26625	3.12849

Source: Bloomberg

to an organization's benefiting from a strengthening of that currency or asset. To a money market dealer, however, a long position is a surplus of borrowings taken in over money lent out (which gives rise to a benefit if that currency weakens rather than strengthens). See **short**.

long-term assets: Assets that are expected to provide benefits and services over a period longer than 1 year.

long-term liabilities: Obligations to be repaid by the firm more than 1 year later.

market maker: Market participant that is committed, explicitly or otherwise, to quoting two-way bid and offer prices at all times in a particular market.

market risk: Risks related to changes in prices of tradable macro-economics variables, such as exchange rate risks.

market trading factors: Issues and circumstances that impact trading strategy and are common to the market as a whole, not to the specific trader or asset.

mark-to-market: The act of revaluing securities to current market values. Such revaluations should include both coupon accrued on the securities outstanding and interest accrued on the cash.

maturity date: Date on which stock is redeemed.

modified restructuring: A term relevant to a credit event in a CDS contract, triggered by debt restructuring undertaken by the reference entity. When a CDS is terminated due to restructuring, the deliverable asset under the terms of the CDS must fall within certain specified types.

negative basis: When the CDS premium of a reference entity is below the asset-swap rate for that same entity.

net present value (NPV): The net present value of a series of cash flows is the sum of the present values of each cash flow (some or all of which may be negative).

no-arbitrage concept: A logic that states that an asset must be priced such that this price presents no opportunity for arbitrage (risk-free) profit. Also known as the "arbitrage-free" price.

nominal amount: See **face value**.

nonperforming: A loan or other asset that is no longer being serviced or has experienced default.

normal: A normal **probability distribution** is a particular distribution assumed to prevail in a wide variety of circumstances, including the financial markets. Mathematically, it corresponds to the probability density function

$$\frac{1}{\sqrt{2\pi}}\, e^{-\frac{1}{2}\phi^2}.$$

notional: In a bond futures contract, the bond bought or sold is a standardized nonexistent notional bond—as opposed to the actual bonds, which are **deliverable** at maturity. **Contracts for differences** also require a notional principal amount on which settlement can be calculated.

NPV: See **net present value**.

outright: Directly, without lien or encumberance.

over the counter (OTC): Strictly speaking, any transaction not conducted on a registered stock exchange. Trades conducted via the telephone between banks, and contracts such as forward rate agreements (FRAs) and non–exchange-traded options, are said to be "over-the-counter" instruments. OTC also refers to nonstandard instruments or contracts traded between two parties; for example, a client with a requirement for a specific risk to be hedged with a tailor-made instrument may enter into an OTC structured option trade with a bank that makes markets in such products. An OTC transaction is one dealt privately between any two parties, with all details agreed between them, as opposed to one dealt on an exchange—for example, a **forward** deal as opposed to a **futures contract**.

paper: Another term for a bond or debt issue.

par: In foreign exchange, when the **outright** and **spot** exchange rates are equal, the **forward swap** is zero or par. When the price of a security is equal to the face value, usually expressed as 100, it is said to be trading at par. A par swap rate is the current market rate for a fixed **interest-rate swap** against **Libor**.

par yield curve: A curve plotting maturity against **yield** for bonds priced at par.

physical settlement: A CDS contract that, on termination, is settled by the deliverable of a loan or bond issued by the reference entity, in exchange for par value of the contract.

plain vanilla: See **vanilla**.

portfolio swap: A CDS that references a basket of reference entities.

positive basis: When the CDS premium for a reference name lies above the asset-swap rate of the same name.

present value (PV): The amount of money that needs to be invested now to achieve a given amount in the future when interest is added. See **time value of money**; **future**.

primary market: The market for new debt, into which new bonds are issued. The primary market is made up of borrowers, investors, and the investment banks that place new debt into the market, usually with their clients. Bonds that trade after they have been issued are said to be part of the **secondary market**.

probability distribution: The mathematical description of how probable it is that the value of something is less than or equal to a particular level.

protection seller: An investor in a CDS contract who provides credit protection to the protection buyer.

PV: See **present value**.

put option: An option to sell the commodity or instrument **underlying** the option.

quanto swap: A **swap** where the payments on one or both legs are based on a measurement (such as the interest rate) in one currency but payable in another currency.

rate of recovery: Estimate of the percentage of the amount exposed to default—in other words, the credit-risk exposure—that is likely to be recovered if a counterparty defaults.

record date: The date at which the share ownership of a company, or holders of debt, is recorded in the company register.

redeem: A security is said to be redeemed when the principal is repaid.

redemption yield: The rate of interest at which all future payments (coupons and redemption) on a bond are discounted so that their total equals the current price of the bond (inversely related to price).

reference asset (reference name, reference obligation, reference credit): The sovereign or corporate entity that is named in a credit derivative contract, on which credit protection is written. Also referred to as "underlying asset." Sometimes refers to a specific asset (loan or bond) of a specified reference name.

reference entity: The corporate entity on which a CDS contract is written.

restructuring: The process of renegotiating the debt of a corporate (or sovereign) borrower.

return on equity: The net earning of a company divided by its equity.

secondary market: The market in instruments after they have been issued. Bonds are bought and sold after their initial issue by the borrower, and the marketplace for this buying and selling is referred to as the secondary market. The new issues market is the **primary market**.

securitization: A capital market transaction described in legal documentation in which illiquid or other assets of a corporation or a financial institution are transformed into a package of securities backed by these assets, through careful packaging, credit enhancements, liquidity enhancements, and structuring. The assets are financed by the issue of liabilities that are termed **asset-backed securities** (ABS) or other such bonds.

security: A financial asset sold initially for cash by a borrowing organization (the "issuer"). The security is often negotiable and usually has a maturity date when it is redeemed.

short: A short position is a surplus of sales over purchases of a given currency or asset, or a situation that naturally gives rise to an organization's benefiting from a weakening of that currency or asset. To a money market dealer, however, a short position is a surplus of money lent out over borrowings taken in (which gives rise to a benefit if that currency strengthens rather than weakens). See **long**.

special: A security that for any reason is sought after in the repo market, thereby enabling any holder of the security to earn incremental income—in excess of the **general collateral (GC)** rate—through lending them via a repo transaction. The repo rate for a special will be below the GC rate, as this is the rate the borrower of the cash is paying in return for supplying the special bond as collateral. An individual security can be in high demand for a variety of reasons—for instance, if there is sudden heavy investor demand for it, or (if it is a benchmark issue) if it is required as a hedge against a new issue of similar maturity paper.

speculation: A term describing speculative market trades, sometimes described as punting or gambling on the future direction of the market.

spot: A deal to be settled on the customary value date for that particular market. In the foreign exchange market, this is for value in two working days' time. Also refers to the zero-coupon interest rate.

standard deviation: A statistic used as a measure of the dispersion or variation in a distribution, equal to the square root of the arithmetic mean of the squares of the deviations from the arithmetic mean.

strike: The strike price or strike rate of an option is the price or rate at which the holder can insist on the underlying transaction being fulfilled. Also known as the "exercise" price.

swap: An exchange of cash flows, such as an interest-rate swap or credit default swap.

synthetic: A package of transactions that is economically equivalent to a different transaction. In the structured finance market, a transaction that replicates some of the economic effects of a cash securitization without recourse to an actual sale of assets, and that involves the use of credit derivatives. For example, the purchase of a **call option** and simultaneous sale of a **put option** at the same **strike** is a synthetic **forward** purchase.

term structure of credit spreads: A plot of the credit spreads for a particular risk level, such as BBB-rated assets, across the term maturity structure.

time value of money: The concept that a future cash flow can be valued as the amount of money that it is necessary to invest now in order to achieve that cash flow in the future. See **present value**; **future**.

trading factors: See **market trading factors**.

underlying: The underlying of a futures or option contract is the commodity or financial instrument on which the contract depends. Thus, underlying for a bond option is the bond; the underlying for a short-term interest-rate futures contract is typically a 3-month deposit.

underwriting: An arrangement by which a company is guaranteed that an issue of debt (bonds) will raise a given amount of cash. Underwriting is carried out by investment banks, which undertake to purchase any part of the debt issue not taken up by the public. A commission is charged for this service.

unexpected default rate: The distribution of future default rates is often characterized in terms of an expected default rate (for example, 0.05%) and a worst-case default rate (for example, 1.05%). The difference between the worst-case default rate and the expected default rate is often termed the "unexpected default" (that is, 1% = 1.05% – 0.05%).

unexpected loss: The distribution of credit losses associated with a derivative instrument is often characterized in terms of an **expected loss** or a **worst-case loss**. The unexpected loss associated with an instrument is the difference between these two measures.

unfunded: A credit derivative contract for which the notional value is not payable on trade inception, hence it requires no funding.

value-at-risk (VAR): Formally, the probabilistic bound of market losses over a given period of time (known as the holding period), expressed in terms of a specified degree of certainty (known as the confidence interval). Put more simply, the VAR is the worst-case loss that would be expected over the holding period within the probability set out by the confidence interval. Larger losses are possible, but with a low probability. For instance, a portfolio whose VAR is $20 million over a 1-day holding period, with a 95% confidence interval, would have only a 5% chance of suffering an overnight loss greater than $20 million.

value date: The date on which a deal is to be consummated. In some bond markets, the value date for coupon accruals can sometimes differ from the settlement date.

vanilla: A vanilla transaction is a straightforward one.

VAR: See **value-at-risk**.

variance (σ^2): A measure of how much the values of something fluctuate around its mean value. Defined as the average of (value – mean)^2. See **standard deviation**.

variance-covariance methodology: Methodology for calculating the **value-at-risk** of a portfolio as a function of the **volatility** of each asset or liability position in the portfolio, and the correlation between the positions.

verification agent: See **calculation agent**.

volatility: The standard deviation of the continuously compounded return on the underlying. Volatility is generally annualized. See **historic volatility; implied volatility**.

worst-case loss: The expected loss amount given default, in the worst-case scenario.

yield: The interest rate that can be earned on an investment, currently quoted by the market or implied by the current market price for the investment—as opposed to the **coupon** paid by an issuer on a security, which is based on the coupon rate and the face value. For a bond, generally the same as yield to maturity unless otherwise specified.

yield curve: Graphical representation of the maturity structure of interest rates, plotting yields of bonds that are all of the same class or credit quality against the maturity of the bonds.

INDEX

A

accrued coupon, 68
adjusted basis, 107–112
adjusted Z-spread, 101,
    104, 107–112
arbitrage opportunities,
    84–85
arbitrage trades
  negative basis, 116
  positive basis, 116–117
asset-backed securities
    (ABS), 67, 89
assets, trading above or
    below par, 68–69
asset swap, 8
  credit default swap basis
    versus, 61–65, 94–96

pricing, 45, 48–50
structure, 13–15
terms, 12
asset-swap spread, 40–41,
    99
  credit default swap basis
    versus, 61–65
average spread, 78–79

B

Banco Bilbao Vizcaya
    Argentaria (BBVA),
    20, 21
basis
  See also credit default
    swap basis

189

PROFESSIONAL
DEVELOPMENT
QUALIFIED ACTIVITY
7 CREDIT HOURS

This book qualifies for seven (7) hours PD credit hours under the guidelines of the CFA Institute Professional Development Program. Please visit www.cfainstitute.org/meresources/pdprogram for more information.

ABOUT BLOOMBERG

Bloomberg L.P., founded in 1981, is a global information services, news, and media company. Headquartered in New York, the company has sales and news operations worldwide.

Bloomberg, serving customers on six continents, holds a unique position within the financial services industry by providing an unparalleled range of features in a single package known as the BLOOMBERG PROFESSIONAL® service. By addressing the demand for investment performance and efficiency through an exceptional combination of information, analytic, electronic trading, and Straight Through Processing tools, Bloomberg has built a worldwide customer base of corporations, issuers, financial intermediaries, and institutional investors.

BLOOMBERG NEWS®, founded in 1990, provides stories and columns on business, general news, politics, and sports to leading newspapers and magazines throughout the world. BLOOMBERG TELEVISION®, a 24-hour business and financial news network, is produced and distributed globally in seven languages. BLOOMBERG RADIO℠ is an international radio network anchored by flagship station BLOOMBERG® 1130 (WBBR-AM) in New York.

In addition to the BLOOMBERG PRESS® line of books, Bloomberg publishes *BLOOMBERG MARKETS®* magazine. To learn more about Bloomberg, call a sales representative at:

London: +44-20-7330-7500
New York: +1-212-318-2000
Tokyo: +81-3-3201-8900

FOR IN-DEPTH MARKET INFORMATION and news, visit the Bloomberg website at **www.bloomberg.com**, which draws from the news and power of the BLOOMBERG PROFESSIONAL® service and Bloomberg's host of media products to provide high-quality news and information in multiple languages on stocks, bonds, currencies, and commodities.

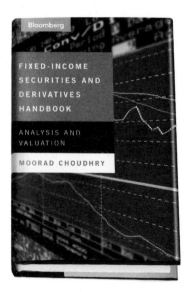

A FRESH VIEW ON FIXED INCOME

As debt market instruments become more complex, financial professionals need to be fully up to speed on how these derivative products and their underlying securities are structured and valued.

Respected practitioner Moorad Choudhry has written a concise and accessible overview of the markets' main elements, the instruments used, and their applications. Analyzing cash and derivative products, he offers unique insights on

- **Bond instruments and interest rate risk**
- **Spot and forward rates**
- **Interest rate modeling**
- **Forwards and futures valuation**
- **Swaps and options**
- **Credit derivatives**
- **Bonds with embedded options**
- **Hybrid securities**
- **Collateralized debt obligations**
- **Yield curve analysis**

With a unique international focus and trading techniques based on the author's personal experience, *Fixed-Income Securities and Derivatives Handbook* is a valuable reference for all bond market participants.

Available in stores or at www.bloomberg.com/books.